NEWBERY
BOOK
CLUB

엄마표 영어로 인풋이 안정된 친구들을 위한

뉴베리 북클럽

NEWBERY BOOK CLUB

24 AWARD-WINNING NOVELS WITH MATRIDUCTIVE LEARNERS

AJ(안재환) 지음

seosawon

Foreword

여러분은 어떤 방법으로 영어를 배웠고, 아이에게는 어떤 방법을 안내해 주고 있나요?

문법 번역식 교수법 → 직접식 교수법 → 청화식 교수법 → 의사소통 교수법. 모국어가 아닌 제2언어 교수법은 시대에 따라 사회적 분위기에 따라 변해왔습니다. 다양한 방식의 교수법이 시도되고 수정되며 1990년대 들어 의사소통 교수법이 지배적인 이론적 모델로 자리잡았지만 대한민국 영어교육 시스템은 문법 번역식에서 크게 변화되지 못했습니다.

1950년대까지 학교에서 외국어를 가르치는 방법으로 선호되었던 문법 번역식 교수법은 현재는 활용하지 않는 고전적 교수법으로 분류합니다. 언어의 유창성과 관계없이 해석하는 방법으로 언어를 가르칩니다. 선생님이 해당 언어에 대한 지식을 학생들에게 전달하는 교수법입니다. 학생들은 먼저, 문법 규칙을 명시적으로 학습하고, 새로운 어휘 목록을 모국어와 함께 암기하고, 문법 활용 연습을 반복하며 텍스트를 해석하는 것에 초점을 맞춘 접근이지요.

언어 학습 성공의 핵심을 학습자가 겪는 언어 경험의 질에 두고 있는 현대적 접근법, 의사소통적 교수법은 이렇게 정의되어 있습니다. "의사소통적 교수법은 원어민의 실제 발화나 글, 즉 구어와 문어에서 사용되는 실제 텍스트를 활용한다. 가르치는 사람 중심인 문법 번역식 교수법과 달리 의사소통적 교수법은 학습자 중심의 읽기, 듣기로 시청각 자료를 매우 풍부하게 제공하는 것이 중요하다. 학습자는 원어민의 실제적인 의사소통 샘플에 많이 노출되어야 한다." 여기에서 놓치면 안 되는 핵심 문구가 '학습자 중심의 읽기, 듣기를 매우 풍부하게 많이 노출' 이것입니다. 읽으면 읽을수록 우리가 이야기하는 '제대로 엄마표 영어'와 많이 닮았습니다. 지금 시대에 통하지 않을 이유가 없는 방법이지요. 또한 지금 시대이기 때문에 통할 수 있는 방법입니다.

장기적인 전략적 원서 읽기가 핵심인 엄마표 영어로 성장하고 있는 아이들은 원음의 영상과 함께하는 '흘려듣기'를 통해 원어민의 실제 발화, 구어에 마음껏 노출되고 있습니다. 원서와 함께하는 '집중듣기'를 통해 한 페이지 한 줄 동화부터 오리지널 고전까지 원어민의 실제적 글, 문어에 풍부하게 많이 노출되고 있습니다. 세상을 만나는 것에 운이 좋은 우리 아이들입니다. 의사소통적 교수법에서 중요한 읽기, 듣기를 위한 풍부한 시청각 자료들이 이토록 차고 넘치는 세상을 이전에 본 적이 없습니다. 우리 세대에게는 의사소통 교수법이 통할 수 없었던 것이 세상 탓도 있었던 거지요.

영어를 누군가 가르쳐주어야 배울 수 있다는 수동적 학습법이 더 이상 불필요한 세상입니다. 아이들 스스로(학습자 중심) 듣고 읽으며 능동적으로 익혀 나갈 수 있는 환경은 이미 갖추어져 있습니다. 언어 학습에 사용되는 테크닉 중 하나인 immersion(몰입)은 언어를 배우는 가장 환상적인 방법이라 평가됩니다. 배우고 있는 언어로 삶의 모든 측면을 경험할 수 있도록, 가능한 한 그 언어로 자신을 둘러싸는 것을 몰입이라 합니다. 언어 몰입이 가능한 방법들입니다. '해당 언어를 사용하는 국가에 거주하고, 해당 언어로 된 영화와 TV 프로그램을 보고, 해당 언어로 된 음악을 듣고, 해당 언어로 된 책을 읽고, 원어민과 대화하기'. 이 중 현지 거주 이외에 우리에게 불가능한 것은 없습니다. 현지에 거주하지 않아도 충분한 인풋 몰입이 충분히 가능한 세상입니다. 제대로 엄마표 영어가 영어 습득을 위한 옳은 길이 될 수 있었던 이유지요. 물론 이런 몰입을 위해서는 장기간 끈기 있는 노력이 필요합니다. 그런데 영어가 평생의 삶에서 도구가 되어줄 수 있다는 보상은 그만한 가치가 있지 않을까요?

여러분은 어떤 방법으로 영어를 배웠고 아이들에게는 어떤 방법을 안내해주고 있나요? 어떤 방법이 지금 시대와 세상에 어울리고 세상이 주는 혜택들까지 누릴 수 있는 방법일까요? 시대와 많이 동떨어진 방법들은 노력의 정도가 커질 수밖에 없고 성공 확률도 떨어지며 결과조차도 시대와 동떨어진 것을 만나게 되는 것은 아닌지 의심해 보셨으면 합니다.

부모 세대의 최선이 아이들에게는 최선이 될 수 없을 정도로 세상은 바뀌었습니다. "내 언어의 한계는 내 세계의 한계를 의미한다." 어느 때보다 이 문장에 공감하지 않을 수 없는 세상이 바로, 지금입니다. 여러분의 세계는 어떤 언어에 갇혀 있을까요? 아이들의 세계는 어떠해야 할까요? 아이들이 성장해서 한계 없는 세상을 만나기 바란다면 공부하는 영어가 더 이상 영어 습득의 해법이 아님을 인정해야 할 겁니다. 방향을 바꿔보십시오. 아이 스스로 익혀 나갈 수 있는 '습득' 방법을 적용하기 최적이고 최고의 환경이니까요.

영어, 잘하고 싶다면 읽어라!

2018년 2월에 출간된 《엄마표 영어 이제 시작합니다》는 초등학교 1학년에 처음 영어를 만난 아이가 그림책부터 고전까지 8년간의 원서읽기를 통해 영어습득 완성을 확인한 경험을 풀어놓은 책입니다. 아이의 영어교육이 좋은 성적을 위한 '학습'이 목표가 아니었습니다. 영어로부터 완벽한 자유를 위한 '습득'이 목표였습니다. 가르치기보다는 더디더라도 아이 스스로 익혀 나가는 길을 선택했습니다. 하지만 그럴 수 있는 방법을 공교육에서도 사교육에서도 찾을 수 없었습니다. 그래서 선택한 것이 엄마표 영어였습니다.

연령만큼 영어 자체 사고력 향상을 위해 '해마다 또래에 맞게 리딩레벨을 업그레이드' 하는 진행이었습니다. 아이의 흥미와 사고에 맞는 영어책 이해가 우리말 책과 다름없이 편해지기까지 만 3년이 걸렸습니다. 4학년에 북레벨 4점대 이상의 단행본 소설을 원서로 읽기 시작하며 아이가 읽을 책을 고르는데 각별히 마음을 썼습니다. 좋은 어휘, 좋은 문장, 좋은 주제를 담은 책과 함께하고 싶어서 5학년 이후 '문학성'을 선정의 핵심 요건으로 삼는 뉴베리(Newbery) 수상작에 집중했습니다.

경험을 나누는 소통 9년 차가 되었습니다. 여타의 외부 도움 없이 《엄마표 영어 이제 시작합니다》 책 한 권을 붙들고 오로지 이 길에서 원하는 목표를 달성하고 '엄마표 영어 졸업'을 선언한 친구가 등장할 정도의 시간이 흘렀습니다. 그 졸업의 소회가 남달랐던 한 친구는 습득된 영어로 모든 학습적 경험의 '주 언어'가 영어가 되었습니다. 원어민 수업? 영어캠프? 1~2년 조기유학? 이런저런 잠깐의 경험이 아닙니다. 미국 하이스쿨 유학을 안방에서 하고 있습니다. 지식을 습득하고 사고를 확장해 나가는 '도구'로 모국어 이외 영어가 더해진 것입니다.

코로나로 인해 세계적으로 온라인 강연이 활발해지면서, 선생님도 함께 수업하는 친구들도 모두 원어민으로 글로벌하게 만날 수 있는 온라인 교육 프로그램들이 폭발적으로 늘었습니다. 아이들 교육에 있어서는 세계가 하나된 세상이 이미 우리 일상에 깊이 들어와 있습니다. 경계도 한계도 없이 지식 습득과 사고 확장을 영어로도 마음껏 누릴 수 있게 되었습니다. 자연스러운 변화로 도래된 것인지 세계적으로 전염병이 대유행하는 팬데믹(Pandemic) 상황으로 인해 그 속도를 가속화시킨 것인지 그건 중요하지 않습니다. 그런 세상이 낯설지 않고 그런 변화된 세상을 마음껏 누리기 위해 내 아이가 든든하게 무장하고 있어야 하는 것이 무엇인지가 중요합니다.

영어교육 방향을 학습이 아니라 습득으로 잡고 이 길에서 애쓰고 있는 친구들이 많아졌다는 것은 반가운 일입니다. 수년 동안의 꾸준한 원서읽기로 영어라는 언어를 '도구'로 사용할 수 있겠다 기대될 정도의 친구들이 늘어가고 있습니다. 그렇게 터를 잘 다져 나가고 있는 친구들을 만나는 행운은 Newbery Book Club(NBC)을 진행하면서였습니다. NBC 기획은 오랜 독자들의 하소연에서 시작되었습니다. 수년간 채워진 인풋으로 고학년에 들어서며 굳이 의도하지 않아도 새어 나오는 아웃풋 조짐이 반가웠지만 채워진 만큼을 Speaking과 Writing으로 적절히 발현시키고 다져줄 수 있는 외부 도움을 찾기가 어렵다고 했습니다. 의외였습니다. 대형 어학원부터 사설학원, 공부방, 개인과외까지 영어 습득을 돕는 외부 도움이 차고 넘치는 세상인데?

원하는 방향은 분명했습니다. 그런데 도움 받을 수 있는 선생님을 가까이에서 찾을 수 없었고 함께하면 시너지가 높을 비슷한 또래의 비슷한 실력을 가진 친구들은 더 찾기 어렵다는 하소연은 이해도 되고 공감도 되었습니다. 원하는 방향은 기존 사교육 시장에서 흔히 볼 수 있는 모습이 아니었습니다. 새로운 커리큘럼을 준비해야 하니 선생님 입장에서는 만만치 않은 시간 투자가 필요합니다. 하지만 잘 만들어 놓은 커리큘럼이라 하더라도 가까이에서 이 정도 수준의 수업을 함께할 친구들을 그룹화하기가 쉽지 않지요. 선생님이 실력이 없어서가 아니라 굳이 그럴 필요가 없어서 하지 않는 수업이니, 찾기 힘든 수업이었던 겁니다.

코로나로 인한 대면 강연 불가로 Zoom 소통이 활발해지며 유사한 고민을 하고 있는 이웃들에게 도움될 수 있는 기획이 떠올랐습니다. 이동 부담이 없다면 수업을 이끌어줄 안성맞춤 선생님도 생각났습니다. 전국 단위 모집이 가능하니 비슷한 또래, 비슷한 수준의 그룹화가 용이할 것 같았습니다. 커리큘럼을 완성하고 참가 희망자를 모집했습니다. 수업에 대해 자세히 설명하고 아이의 동의를 받는 것이 우선이라 못 박았지요. 그럼에도 불구하고 엄마의 욕심이 전부인 신청도 일부 있었습니다. 그런 신청을 제외한다 해도 아웃풋 발현이 기대되는 탄탄한 인풋을 채워 놓은 친구들이 많다는 것을 확인하며 놀랍고 반가웠습니다. 대전을 비롯해서 서울 경기 쪽은 물론이고 부산, 거제, 포항, 경주, 김해, 광주, 속초 등등. 그야말로 전국구 신청에 일부 바다 건너 타국에 계신 분들도 보였습니다. 온라인 수업의 장점이었지요. 기수가 이어질수록 참가 희망 경쟁은 치열해졌습니다.

일주일에 한 번 아이들과 진행하는 90분은 특별했습니다. 단순 질문에 단순한 답을 채워 나가며 무언가를 기억하기 위한 시간이 아니었습니다. 같은 책을 읽은 또래들과 모여 책을 읽고 갖게 된 각자의 생각을 말로 풀어놓는데 선생님은 교통정리만 해주면 되었습니다. 억지로라도 집어넣을 수 있는 인풋 수업이 아니었습니다. 채워진 만큼 끄집어내는 아웃풋 발현 유도 수업이었습니다. 사고력이 바탕되지 않는 아웃풋은 금방 바닥이 드러나게 되어 있는데 선정한 책들은 북레벨도 주제도 만만치 않은 뉴베리 수상작들이었습니다. 일주일에 한 권씩, 한 기수에 24권을 함께했습니다.

이토록 멋진 이야기가 담긴 책들을 학습을 위한 교재로 사용하고 싶지 않았습니다. 한 권의 책을 소화하는 데 여러 날이 필요한 친구들이 아니었습니다. 모국어가 아닌 언어로 쓰여진, 좋은 책으로 공식 인정받은, 상당한 난이도의 책을 '원문 그대로' 글쓴이가 전하고자 하는 것을 받아들이고 이해하고 공감할 수 있는 친구들입니다. 그래서 매주 새로운 책으로 함께하는 것이 가능했습니다.

영어 수준은 이미 엄마를 능가했으니 답지도 없는 Before Class 준비도 After Class 과제도 오로지 혼자 힘으로 해결해야 하는데 수업 형식도 과제도 피드백도 낯설기만 한 쉽지 않은 수업이었습니다. 그런데 힘들어도 놓고 싶지 않은 이 수업의 매력이 무엇이었을까요? 말을 물가로 끌고 갈 수는 있어도 물을 억지로 마시게 할 수는 없고, 놀아보라 멍석을 깔아주어도 멍석 위에서 주인공이 되어 놀 것인지 멍석 주위에서 구경꾼이 될 것인지 누구도 등 떠밀 수 없다는데 어디에 맑은 물이 있는지 알려주면 뚜벅뚜벅 자기 걸음으로 걸어가 시원하게 들이킬 준비가 된 아이들이 NBC 친구들이었습니다.

NBC는 시작하면 최소 6개월부터 10개월까지 지속되는 커리큘럼입니다. 처음 기획할 때는 7기까지 이어질 것이라 예상하지 못했습니다. 어머님들께서 강연장을 찾아주셨을 때 미취학이었던 아이들이 수업을 함께한 것이 신기했습니다. 기수가 이어질수록 발전하는 아이들의 놀라운 실력에 입이 다물어지지 않았습니다. 그만큼 원서읽기를 통한 영어 성장이 자연스럽고 대세가 된 상황이 반가웠습니다. 이 길이 영어 습득을 위한 옳은 길이라는 확신은 더욱 단단해졌습니다.

많은 분들이 관심 주시고 참여해 주셨던 NBC가 7기 수업이 종료되며 잠정 중단됩니다. 학년 제한을 두었던 모집이어서 학년이 되기만을 기다리셨다는 이웃님들, 인터뷰 재도전을 기다리셨다는 이웃님들 모두가 중단 소식에 너무 아쉬워하셔서 죄송한 마음입니다. 원하시는 분들은 많은데 수업을 접어야 하는 것이 기획한 사람으로서도 아쉬워서 NBC 수업이 어떻게 진행되었는지 글로 모두 담았습니다. 함께 모여 생각을 나눌 수 없다는 것이, 과제에 대한 피드백으로 Writing

발전에 도움을 줄 수 없다는 것이 안타깝지만 원서 읽기를 통한 영어 습득의 장기 계획에 적절히 활용될 수 있기를 기대합니다.

아이의 영어 첫 시작이 '누리보듬식' 엄마표 영어였다고 전해주는 독자들에게 무거운 책임을 느낍니다. 주시는 어떤 글에도 같이 고민하고 도움이 되었으면 하는 생각을 전하는 것을 소홀히 하지 않는 이유입니다. 7세 또는 8세에 한 페이지 한 줄 문장의 동화 보기로 영어를 처음 시작한 친구들이 고학년이 되었고 세계적으로 인정받은 소설들을 원문 그대로 읽으며 감동받고 있습니다. 이제 이 친구들은 지식을 습득하고 사고를 확장해 나가는 언어로 모국어뿐만 아니라 영어도 도구로 사용할 수 있게 되었습니다. 그 도구가 날카로운 쓰임이 될 수 있도록 잘 다듬어가는 단계에서 활용할 수 있기를 바라며 두 권의 책을 영어 원문으로 출간하는 모험을 해봤습니다.

《English Grammar for Matriductive Learners》,《Newbery Book Club_24 Award-Winning Novels with Matriductive Learners》. 아이들을 이끌어주고 그 시간을 글로 정리해준 AJ에게 고마움을 전합니다. 아직은 수요와 시장이 제한되어 있음을 잘 알고 계시면서 두 권의 출판을 위해 애써주신 서사원 출판사에 깊이 감사드립니다.

선생님과 수업은 끝이 났지만 지속적으로 매주 만나 아이들끼리 북클럽을 이어가는 팀들이 많습니다. 같은 책을 읽고 생각을 나누고 나눈 생각을 정리하는 것에 익숙해진 친구들이 꾸준히 책과 함께할 수 있도록 관계 유지를 위해 적극적으로 지원해주신 어머님들께 감사드립니다.

마지막으로 아이의 영어 성장에 안정을 넘어 완성의 단계까지 리드했을 모든 어머님들께 경의를 표합니다. 이 길을 선택함에 있어 많이 불안했을 시작, 그리고 수많은 시행착오에 마음 흔들렸을 초기 단계를 현명히 넘기느라 애쓰셨을 시간들에 위로와 축하도 전하고 싶습니다.

2023년 4월
누리보듬

Preface

The Birth of the Newbery Book Club

The sensational saga to the birth of the Newbery Book Club was meticulously unraveled in my previous book, <English Grammar for Matriductive Learners>, published June 2022. I quote my writing there to do the same here.

Benjamin Franklin once said, "Diligence is the mother of good luck." What he probably meant was to work hard and eventually luck will find its way. However, the exact opposite happens more often in life—good luck comes to you first, and *then* you realize you have been preparing for it your entire life.

If someone had told me a few years back that I'd be running one of the most desired English classes in Korea, I'd have probably laughed it off. Even now, to have students line up and take interviews to join my class feels unreal. And, to be requested to teach English grammar when I've never had proper grammar education myself—I mean, that's ridiculous, isn't it? But now, having taught English for over a year, I realize that I've *always* been preparing for this—this is the *fruit* of my journey through the English language.

Back when I was in elementary school, the plague of private English education was blossoming in Korea. With the continuing reign of English as the *lingua franca* since the 18th century, English had already become a mandatory subject in Korean schools long before I entered one. However, there was one problem: English (and any other language, for that matter) is too broad of a topic to master at school. Therefore, as I entered elementary school, private institutes offering supplementary English education began appearing left and right. By the time I progressed to second grade, most of my classmates were already enrolled in these private institutes. However, my mother did not approve of their teaching methods—these institutes only focused on perfecting their students' ability to provide the correct answer to English exam questions. My mother regarded this type of education absolutely unacceptable for the acquisition of any language. Hence, she decided to employ her own plans to help me conquer English. And now, almost fifteen years later, I am the product of my mother's pioneering research and application of what's called, the "Matriductive* Way" of learning English: an approach of acquiring English at home wherein *the mother* is heavily involved in the planning, the acting, and the instructing of the child.

The crux of the Matriductive Way is to expose the child to luscious English literature and speech. Even as a little child, a plethora of ostensibly appealing starter tools for English was available in Korea (e.g., workbooks about phonetics and phonology). However, my mother had a strong disapproval toward these materials—she considered them too technical and unnecessarily complicated. She instead handed me *English books* and *videos*. At the age of eight, I picked up my first English book, and throughout my later elementary school years, I ploughed through countless English children's novels (mostly Newbery-awarded and -nominated books). After I graduated elementary school, I found myself enjoying more sophisticated "classic" English novels, such as <Brave New World>, <1984>, <The Invisible Man>, and <A Tale of Two Cities>. At the same time, my go-to leisure activity was watching English shows and movies on the Disney Channel and Nickelodeon.

An astral crossing of lucks sent me to Australia and placed me in an undergraduate course at the age of sixteen. Let me repeat: I got admitted into a university in an English-speaking country at sixteen. Moreover, my performance there was exceptional— enough to earn me a seat in the Vice Chancellor's Merit List. All this gave my mother enough confidence to spare her knowledge of the Matriductive Way in the form of a book. A surprising number of Korean parents were inspired by it, and they decided to apply the strategy on their children. Several years later, I came to the pleasant realization that countless Korean children were following the same process whereby I learned English.

Then, just about a year ago, I was offered to lead some of these children in a book club—I was given a chance to discuss Newbery books with Korean students who have been following the Matriductive Way. The premise was this: children who've practiced the Matriductive Way have never had a chance to *speak* in English. Furthermore, they've never had a chance to test their English skills within a *class setting*. And what better class to run with these children than a *book club*? (Recall that the core of the Matriductive Way is to expose children to various forms of English media, including *books*.)

● A word that I've created and used in this book to refer to the particular method of learning English explained in text. *Matri-* = mother; *-duc-* = to lead

The only problem was this: I had neither taught nor had been taught English before. However, my worry soon disappeared when I was handed the Newbery books the parents wanted me to discuss. They were the exact books I read while growing up—I was delighted to see them again! In hindsight, of course they would be the same books. The Newbery Medal has been being annually awarded to the "most distinguished contribution to American literature for children" by the American Library Association *for over a hundred years*. Even after decades, the Newbery-awarded books would remain as great picks for children. Books never change; only the reader does.

Reading the books again, I realized that I *did* change. Unlike when I was a kid, I could comprehend the books more thoroughly—I could understand their lessons; I could read between the lines. The more I read the books, the better idea I got on how to run the class. And the more I read the books, the more I wanted to discuss their messages.

In the end, I decided to set the focus of my class on those *messages* the books were trying to send. In other words, I decided to place more emphasis on the *ideas* the books contained, rather than their respective plots. I didn't want to turn my class into a memory game of remembering little details from the story. Instead, I wanted to guide the students to the lessons the books were trying to give, the ideas they were trying to convey, and the messages they were trying to deliver. After I had a clear idea of what I wanted to do, I accepted the offer and started preparing for the class.

Thus, the "Newbery Book Club" was born—one book a class, one class a week, twenty-four books in total (i.e., six months total). Having marked its first anniversary not too long ago, I've already had the honor to lead countless students within the book club. And now, students line up to take interviews just to have a chance at entering my class—how profound! Every class was memorable, every student improved their English substantially, and most importantly, we formed a strong bond. To see the students mature in their thoughts under my instruction flooded me with unique emotions that I *know* I won't be able to experience in any other way.

This book unveils my comprehensive breakdown and piercing questions on the twenty-four books in the Newbery Book Club. The transcript has been prepared entirely by myself; each literature analysis will inevitably contain mild subjectivity and bias. Yet I am confident that the level of preciseness and completeness equipped with this book will be challenging to find elsewhere. I hope my exhaustive studies assist you in capitalizing on every available experience in each book (and other great literature you will come across in the future).

Breaking Down Each Book

Let me first illustrate the vibrant angles of analysis I offer in this book. Each chapter consists of the following six sections: *Plot Introduction*, *Themes*, *Questions*, *Vocabulary Exercise*, *Paragraph Write-up Exercise*, and *Bibliography*.

The *Plot Introduction* roughly outlines the book's story. Note, however, that it markedly contrasts with a summary. As the name suggests, the *Plot Introduction* merely cues you into the book; it does not provide the 'full picture.' I have ensured to exclude all potential spoilers from the *Plot Introductions*. I arranged my writing to grant you only a vague idea of the book's scenario and motifs. I have also limited the length of every *Plot Introduction* to 300 words. Remember that solely consulting my *Plot Introduction* is never a replacement for reading the original book.

The following section, *Themes*, is an ambitious scrutiny of the themes, motifs, backgrounds, and possible discussions dissolved within the story. From major topics that span the entire story to bitesize ideas found in its small parts—every noteworthy concept will be examined in this section. While the *Themes* section intrinsically focuses on the salient purports and messages of the book, these are not the only items on its agenda. Any point of interest and relevance is included in this section—be it the historical significance of the novel's setting, the inspiration for the story (referred from the author interview), and related facts and statistics. Unfortunately (as I remark in a few chapters), it is simply impossible to discuss all the nuances of a book within my humble writing. You must perform your *own* investigations to absorb every book fully; my analysis will give you a good starting point.

The next three sections: *Questions*, *Vocabulary Exercise*, and *Paragraph Write-up Exercise* are elements handled in class (live). I will detail them later.
Finally, the *Bibliography* section lists the sources I consulted while preparing the chapter. Data and information from the materials were incorporated into (primarily) the *Themes* section or the *Questions* section.

Active Class: The Concept

Of the elements in each chapter, the sections: *Questions*, *Vocabulary Exercise*, and

Paragraph Write-up Exercise are actively engaged in class. The *Questions* part provides the inquiries (on the novel) handled in class. The *Vocabulary Exercise* and *Paragraph Write-up Exercise* present the activities given as homework afterward.

Active Class: The Questions

Before I disclose the nature of my analytic questions, let me briefly discuss the "Summary and First Impressions" part. The "Summary and First Impressions" part opens every class. Before each class, my students prepare a summary of the entire book. At the start of every class, the students present their summaries in an arbitrary order. I then provide my remarks on each student's summary—including, perhaps, critical parts they've missed out on (i.e., pivotal events from the book they should have mentioned in their summary), parts they've interpreted inappropriately (i.e., interpretations that are contrasting to the book's message), and parts that would have been better left out (i.e., parts that are unimportant or irrelevant to the overall plot). Since my students can allocate as much time as they want in preparing their summaries, placing the "Summary and First Impressions" as the opening part of the class imbues even the timidest students with the confidence to speak up. It helps them to relax; it gets them in the mood to talk. After every student presents their summary, I ask for their general opinion on the story. Some students acknowledge the genre of the book, some mention their favorite part from the book, and so on.

The summary section changes in the second half of the book club—instead of the full book summary, I only require each student to provide their favorite part from the book. This empirical amendment was because my students comfortably produced high-quality summaries after twelve classes, and—more importantly—the "Summary and First Impressions" part took up too much time. Hence, I simplified the section.

Now, I shall enlighten you on the delectable inquiries offered in my class. As per the architecture of the Newbery Book Club, this book is divided into two major parts. The first part—which covers the first three months (i.e., the first half) of the book club—is *story-oriented*. The first half was designed to hone my students' skills to identify the important parts and distinguish them from the unimportant parts of the story. Novelists often avoid weaving their stories exclusively around their central message. While this would allow the readers to understand their motives more clearly, doing so often results in a mundane, monotonous plot. Therefore, authors include bitesize side stories and extra bits of details to create luscious stories. This satiates our appetite for a tasteful story but leaves the main message obscure. Hence, everyone needs to polish their ability to screen the critical parts of the story—only then can one firmly grasp the themes and lessons of the book.

Throughout the first half, questions asking for essential details from the plot comprise most of each class. The exhaustive analysis of the story is followed by the consideration of the leading characters in the book (their personalities and attributes). Finally, each class is concluded with an investigation of the book's principal themes and messages through a series of related personal questions. These last few "theme questions" comprise the only section that requires personal input during the first half of the book club.

The second part of this book—which covers the latter three months (i.e., the second half) of the Newbery Book Club—is *theme-oriented*. Having polished their "plot screening skill" for three months, many of my students could comfortably identify and recall critical plot points on their own. Subsequently, we could redirect our focus to the ideas and themes of the books (away from their stories) in the second half.

Throughout this second part, questions inquiring about one's thoughts comprise most of each class. The questions no longer demand evoking information from the story; they ask for the reader's opinion on parts of the story or the story as a whole. Here, you'll encounter considerations like: "Why did Character A follow Plan 1 instead of Plan 2?" "What would have happened had Character A pursued Plan 2 instead?" and "Why did Character A hold the particular attitude to Character B?" In addition (similar to the "theme questions" above), countless philosophical questions will offer comprehensive explorations of the central themes and messages of the books. To summarize, this second part will more faithfully represent a book discussion club.

As you work through the "Discussion Questions" in the second half, you will encounter my additional input in one of three forms: "Chew on this," "Reminder," or "Hint." Consult the following list for more information on each aid.

- "**Chew on this**" suggests you consider what follows. What comes after "Chew on this" is often not necessary to answer the corresponding question. Most of the time, it will consist of intriguing information or news related to the question (for you to "chew on").
- "**Reminder**" summarizes the relevant section from the original book that helps or is required to answer the corresponding question. It is to help you recall the related event, just in case you have forgotten.
- "**Hint**" offers some ideas to consult while answering the corresponding question. It is

generally included for broad questions to point you in the right direction.

Active Class: The Vocabulary Exercise and the Paragraph Write-up Exercise

After each class, two exercises are given as homework—the *Vocabulary Exercise* and the *Paragraph Write-up Exercise*. During the first half of the book club, the *Vocabulary Exercise* consisted of creating sentences by separately incorporating ten words and phrases used in the book. Students were given ten words and phrases from each book; for each word, they were to construct a sentence that displays efficient usage of the word. By the end, each student would have written ten original sentences. As you attempt this section, you must produce sentences that hold independent significance. In other words, each sentence you create should be unquestionably coherent and complete on its own; it should not require additional sentences to provide further context. Should you feel this is challenging to ensure with only a single sentence, you can write more (though I recommend a maximum of two sentences). In addition, as far as this exercise is concerned, try to match your use of the word to the book. A single word may hold more than one meaning. For clarity, I directed my students to follow the book's usage (of the words and phrases) closely when drafting their own sentences. Try to do so yourself.

Next, the *Paragraph Write-up Exercise* instructs you to answer a series of questions that probe the book's principal theme(s) by writing a paragraph. Every time, you will encounter multiple questions that address the book's central theme(s). It is imperative that you answer in a *single paragraph*; you are *not* to answer the questions separately. Each exercise will ask one 'principal question (usually the first)' followed by several 'connected questions.' The 'connected questions' will guide you in constructing your paragraph answer—they hint at key points I would discuss if I received the 'principal question.' As an inexperienced writer (yet), you may get lost while contemplating which ideas to incorporate into your answer. To help you, I propose ideas to consider through the 'connected questions.' Once again, remember to include your answers to all the questions in a single paragraph. I also define a "paragraph" in every *Paragraph Write-up Exercise* section. If you are unsure what a "paragraph" is, refer to the corresponding section.

The *Vocabulary Exercise* evolves in the second half of the book club. After three months of the sentence-writing *Vocabulary Exercise*, most of my students had become comfortable creating separate sentences from the words and phrases. Hence, I decided to step it up by assigning them to produce their own "creative writing" using the ten words and phrases. I allowed the students to choose the topic and structure of their "creative writing"—as long as it displayed efficient uses of the words and phrases, anything from original stories to diary entries was permitted. For this exercise, it seemed nefarious to enforce using all ten words and phrases. Hence, I set the minimum to *seven*—each student had to weave at least seven (of the ten) words and phrases into their writing. This homework sincerely enhanced my students' vocabulary range and skills. As you attempt this section, try to challenge yourself to various styles of writing. Or, try to compose a continuing story using the vocabulary sets from several consecutive books. As ambitious as this exercise is, you will be thoroughly entertained while attempting to produce fascinating pieces of writing. Meanwhile, the *Paragraph Write-up Exercise* remains unchanged. Refer to my explanation above regarding this exercise.

Throughout the active Newbery Book Club, I provided feedback on every student's homework. Regarding the *Vocabulary Exercise*, I commented on inappropriate uses of the words and phrases and critical grammatical errors. For the *Paragraph Write-up Exercise*, I assessed the ethical correctness of the student's answer as well as its alignment with the book's message. I also noted the structure of their paragraph—its coherency and clarity—and provided writing tips whenever possible.

Outlook

Reading is—and should be—a unique experience for everyone. Just as two people are never the same, two people's reading experiences of a book can never be the same either. Different people have different thoughts and interpret a text differently. However, novice readers require guidance—especially regarding complex literature. Newbery-awarded and -nominated books include sophisticated undertones, hidden messages, and calculated metaphors. These may not be obvious to young, aspiring readers; they might miss the full experience offered by each of these brilliant books. I hope this book can assist those pupils in advancing their wisdom through the priceless tool: *books*. In a broader sense, I hope this book can inspire the general audience to appreciate reading and enlighten them on how a single book can hold so many incredible ideas and powerful messages.

Today a reader, tomorrow a leader
- Margaret Fuller, American journalist, and activist

A Guide to This Book

How is the Book Structured?

This book investigates **the twenty-four books included in my Newbery Book Club**. Each chapter examines **one novel**. Each chapter consists of the following **nine sections**.

1. Title Page

2. Plot Introduction

3. Themes

4. Questions

5. Vocabulary Exercise

6. Paragraph Write-up Exercise

7. Bibliography

8. About the Author

9. Other Books by the Author

What Does Each Part Mean?

Let me clarify the context of **the six main parts** of a chapter.

Plot Introduction

Do you love stories? Well, strap yourself in because this book is a three-in-one package! Our hero is Stanley Yelnats, a slightly overweight boy who continuously gets bullied at school. Whenever something unfortunate happens to Stanley, he blames his "curse of bad luck," passed on by his great-great-grandfather, Elya Yelnats. Ages ago, Elya received a pig from Madame Zeroni, his gypsy friend. Elya sought to gift the pig to the woman he wished to marry. In exchange for the pig, h

and sing her a lullaby. However,

bad luck on Elya and the gener

The *Plot Introduction* presents **a synopsis of the novel's plot**. It *cannot* replace reading the original book. It is merely to spark your interest—to motivate you to read the book. A *Plot Introduction* is 300 words at max.

Themes

The most noteworthy theme in *Holes* is *the role of fate in real-life events*. The "curse" of Stanley being in the wrong place at the wrong time (which leads to him getting accused of stealing Clyde Livingston's s.....es) ...... like a twisted joke of destiny. The a....... explicitly disclosing whether fate a...... of fact, the "curse" is never confirm....... the book just incredible coinciden....

> The *Themes* section contains **every compelling, thought-provoking narrative regarding the novel.** Ideas you might encounter in a *Themes* section include the main message/lesson of the book, the historical event weaved into the story, and the social/scientific significance of the plot.

Questions

① **Summary and First Impressions**

    A. Can you give a short summary of the story?

    B. What do you think about the story? Do you like it?

    C. Which characteristic...... you do not?

> The *Questions* section provides **the penetrating questions I prepared and discussed within the Newbery Book Club.**

In the first half, my class focuses on *the plot*; most of the questions inquire about the book's story.

② **Story Questions**

    A. Why does Stanley and his family have a curse of bad luck? Can you explain the story of Stanley's great-great-grandfather, Elya Yelnats?

    B. Why was Sam killed...... 'Wh......

    C. Why did Katherine be...... outlaw?

> The "Story Questions" require you to recall **critical details from the plot**.

③ Character Questions

A. At the start of the story, how is Stanley like? Is he shy and quiet or outgoing and loud? How is Stanley's self-esteem—is it high or low?

B. What characteristic does Stanley's family share?

C. How does Stanley's personality change as the story unfolds? How does meeting Zero change Stanley? Would you say he grows up/becomes more mature?

D. How is Zero like? Does

E. How is Zero like in his fri
Stanley?

The "Character Questions" investigate **the characteristics and relationships of the characters** in the book.

④ Theme Questions

A. Many events in the book seems to occur as a result of coincidence. Do you think the events are actually mere coincidence or fate? Do you believe in fate in real life?

B. The friendship between Stanley and Zero is key to the overall plot. They both change massively by the end of the book and benefit substantially from each other. Do you think friends
you have a friend who h

The "Theme Questions" ask for **your thoughts on the central message(s)/lesson(s)** of the book.

In the second half, my class focuses on *the implications*; the questions involve ideas written in the *Themes* section.

② Discussion Questions

A. Just like in the book, many real-life human activities often threaten wildlife (big or small, legal or illegal, and intentional or unintentional). What do you think we can do to protect wildlife?

　i. What can you do, as

　ii. What should a gover

　iii. Why is it important to

The "Discussion Questions" approach the book from **various perspectives**—they will prompt you to consider the characters' actions and thoughts, the historical event weaved into the story, and the novel's social/scientific significance.

To help you answer the questions and expand your knowledge, I provide **additional input** to some questions. They will be in one of the following **three forms**.

Chew on this

"So my mom had a vacuum cleaner that she loved, and she passed away in 2009. In the last year of her life, she kept on saying 'what's going to happen to the vacuum cleaner when I'm gone?' And I was like, 'why are we worried about the vacuum cleaner? There are bigger things to worry about,' but when she died, I did as I promised her I would do. I took the [vac]
Then, the spring after my [...]
house, draped dramatical[...]
when I got close to him, a[...]

> "Chew on this" suggests you consider what follows. What comes after "Chew on this" is often not necessary to answer the corresponding question. Most of the time, it will consist of **intriguing information or news related to the question** (for you to "chew on").

Reminder

William wanted to be addressed specifically as "William Spiver" so he could have the same name as his biological father, William, yet would be distinguished (because of the additional part, "Spiver"). His stepfather, Tyrone, called him Billy "one time too many," which "cracked" W[...]
mother found out, she got[...]
Tootie.

> "Reminder" summarizes the relevant section from the original book that helps or is required to answer the corresponding question. It is to **help you recall the related event**, just in case you have forgotten.

Hint

Comparing Leigh's first few letters to his later ones will reveal one or two obvious changes to his writing. Ho[...]
his sixth-grade year as we[...]
vocabulary choices, and hi[...]

> "Hint" offers some ideas to consult while answering the corresponding question. It is generally included for broad questions to **point you in the right direction**.

The *Vocabulary Exercise* is an activity to attempt after answering all the *Questions*.

Vocabulary Exercise

Instructions

These are some words and phrases used in *Holes*. Write each of their definition in English. Then, for each word, create your own sentence including that word. Be mindful that one word can have multiple meanings or be used in more than one way. Carefully consider how the words and phrases were used in the original book, and try to use each word/phrase the same way as how the book used it.

Words & Phrases

authenticated	custody
hallucination	warden

You are given **ten words and phrases** used in the original book. You are to either 1) **write ten separate sentences** using each word/phrase once or 2) **write a paragraph with the topic of your choice** using at least seven of the words/phrases. Detailed instructions are available in every chapter.

The *Paragraph Write-up Exercise* is another activity to attempt after answering all the *Questions*.

Paragraph Write-up Exercise

Instructions

Write a short paragraph expressing your thoughts about the following questions. There are multiple questions to guide you arrange your thoughts and form your answer. Be sure to answer all the questions within a sing...

A "paragraph" is a collection of ... convey a single idea throughout. ... coherently deliver your thoughts t... sentences.

You are asked **a series of questions** regarding the original book's central message(s) and lesson(s). You are to **compile your answers (to all the questions) into a single paragraph**—your answers must not be divided into separate lines. Detailed instructions are available in every chapter.

Question

How does Stanley's personaliti...
that way and which characters ...

Bibliography

1 – "The Holocaust" from *History.com* (https://www.history.com/topics/world-war-ii/the-holocaust)

2 – "Holocaust" from *Encyclop*

> The *Bibliography* section provides **the materials I consulted** while preparing the chapter. Information and data gathered from these sources would (generally) have been included in either the *Themes* or the *Questions* (my "additional input") section.

How Do I Use This Book?

I recommend reading the books in order, though it's not mandatory. However, you **must work through the first twelve books before moving on to the latter twelve**. The questions in the first half are designed to prepare you for those in the second half.

The best approach to conquering a chapter would be the following:

1. Read the *Plot Introduction*.

2. Read the original novel.

3. Attempt the *Questions*.

4. Read the *Themes* section (and, optionally, consult the materials in the *Bibliography*).

5. Attempt the *Questions* once again.

6. Attempt the *Vocabulary Exercise* and *Paragraph Write-up Exercise*.

Contents

Holes

by Louis Sachar

Published	1998 (1999 Newbery Medal)
ATOS Book Level	4.6
Lexile	660L
Word Count	47079

Plot Introduction

Do you love stories? Well, strap yourself in because this book is a three-in-one package! Our hero is Stanley Yelnats, a slightly overweight boy who continuously gets bullied at school. Whenever something unfortunate happens to Stanley, he blames his "curse of bad luck," passed on by his great-great-grandfather, Elya Yelnats. Ages ago, Elya received a pig from Madame Zeroni, his gypsy friend. Elya sought to gift the pig to the woman he wished to marry. In exchange for the pig, he promised Zeroni to take her up a mountain on the pig's back and sing her a lullaby. However, Elya failed to fulfill this promise, and Zeroni placed a curse of bad luck on Elya and the generations to come. Onto story number two: 110 years ago, the affair between Kate Barlow, a white woman, and Sam, a black man, was the buzz around Town Green Lake. Back then, racism still plagued the town, and this affair enraged the townspeople. They hunted Sam down, and he met his demise while crossing the Green Lake. Following this event, the lake dried up, and Kate turned into an outlaw—she even robbed Stanley's great-grandfather once! On her deathbed, she hinted that she had buried all her treasures at the bottom of the Green Lake. Back to the present: Stanley is sent to Camp Green Lake—a place for juvenile felons—as he gets accused of stealing a famous basketball star's shoes. There, he is forced to dig holes at the lakebed every day. The Warden claims the digging is for the inmates to build character, but Stanley soon realizes she is looking for something. Will Stanley survive the scorching heat and the deadly lizards of Camp Green Lake and safely recover his great-grandfather's treasures?

Themes

The most noteworthy theme in *Holes* is *the role of fate in real-life events*. The "curse" of Stanley being in the wrong place at the wrong time (which leads to him getting accused of stealing Clyde Livingston's shoes) and the reunification of Yelnats and Zeroni—it all feels like a twisted joke of destiny. The author gracefully dissolves this theme into his book by never explicitly disclosing whether fate actually had a hand in any of the book's events. (As a matter of fact, the "curse" is never confirmed either.) This begs the question: are all of the events in the book just incredible coincidences, or does fate have a play?

Next, we must discuss *the power of friendship* and the consequent *transformations* of the individuals involved. Throughout the book, our protagonist goes through a variety of changes, both mentally and physically. Not only does he get fit from all the digging, but his personality also takes a brilliant turn for the positive. Most of his changes come about from his excellent friendship with Zero. To many, one of the most impressive moments in the book was when Stanley stood up for Zero against the bullies of Camp Green Lake. Remember: Stanley practically had no friends in school before joining the camp. The book sure leaves the readers a lot to think about how a good friendship can transform a person 180 degrees.

Some minor themes include *never losing hope* and *nature*. In spite of their curse, Stanley's family never loses hope and eventually gets rewarded for their positive attitude and perseverance at the end of the book. In other news, Sam's onions at the top of the mountain play a key role in saving Stanley and Zero's lives. First, they survived off the onions for two weeks while they were away from camp, and they also avoided the attack of the deadly lizards when they were having a standoff against the Warden for Stanley's briefcase. Remember kids: eat your vegetables.

Questions

① Summary and First Impressions

A. Can you give a short summary of the story?

B. What do you think about the story? Do you like it?

C. Which characteristics do you think you share with Stanley? Which do you think you do not?

② Story Questions

A. Why does Stanley and his family have a curse of bad luck? Can you explain the story of Stanley's great-great-grandfather, Elya Yelnats?

B. Why was Sam killed? Why did the townspeople want to kill Sam?

C. Why did Katherine become an outlaw? What did she do after she became an outlaw?

D. When did the Green Lake dry up?

E. What does Stanley do every day at Camp Green Lake? Why did the Warden want the kids to dig holes at the lakebed?

F. What does Stanley teach Zero and what does Zero do in return? What effect does this have on the story near the end?

G. What was at the top of the big mountain Stanley and Zero climbed up? How were they able to survive for more than a week?

H. How was it possible for Stanley to lift his curse at the top of the big mountain?

I. What did Stanley and Zero find in the hole after returning to the camp?

J. Why was Stanley let go from the camp?

K. How was Stanley able to keep the suitcase to himself?

L. What was in the suitcase and how did its contents help Stanley and Zero?

A. At the start of the story, how is Stanley like? Is he shy and quiet or outgoing and loud? How is Stanley's self-esteem—is it high or low?

B. What characteristic does Stanley's family share?

C. How does Stanley's personality change as the story unfolds? How does meeting Zero change Stanley? Would you say he grows up/becomes more mature?

D. How is Zero like? Does he bear any similarities to Stanley in his characteristics?

E. How is Zero like in his friendship with Stanley? Is he loyal? Does he stand up for Stanley?

F. What characteristics do Stanley and Zero share? Also, how are they different?

G. How does Zero's personality change as the story unfolds? How does his friendship with Stanley affect him?

④ Theme Questions

A. Many events in the book seems to occur as a result of coincidence.
   Do you think the events are actually mere coincidence or fate? Do you believe in fate in real life?

B. The friendship between Stanley and Zero is key to the overall plot. They both change massively by the end of the book and benefit substantially from each other. Do you think friends can change each other's personalities and behaviors? Do you have a friend who has affected you in such impactful ways?

Vocabulary Exercise

Instructions

These are some words and phrases used in *Holes*. Write each of their definition in English. Then, for each word, create your own sentence including that word. Be mindful that one word can have multiple meanings or be used in more than one way. Carefully consider how the words and phrases were used in the original book, and try to use each word/phrase the same way as how the book used it.

Words & Phrases

| authenticated | custody | defective | initiate | legitimate |
| hallucination | warden | refuge | tedious | perseverance |

Sentences from the book

Here are the sentences from the original book that contains the given words and phrases. Only use these as reference and do not write the same sentences for your exercise.

authenticated: "It was not **authenticated**," the Warden said. / "**Authenticated**? It was signed by the judge who sentenced him."

custody: "The boys in my **custody** have proven themselves dangerous to society."

defective: He wondered if he had a **defective** shovel.

initiate: The A.G. will most likely **initiate** an investigation.

legitimate: "How do I know it's **legitimate**?"

hallucination: "He's been suffering from **hallucinations** and delirium."

warden: The person you've got to worry about is the **Warden**.

refuge: When he was asked how he had lived so long, he said he "found **refuge** on God's thumb."

tedious: The reader probably still has some questions, but unfortunately, from here on in, the answers tend to be long and **tedious**.

perseverance: Stanley's father was smart and had a lot of **perseverance**.

Paragraph Write-up Exercise

Instructions

Write a short paragraph expressing your thoughts about the following questions. There are multiple questions to guide you arrange your thoughts and form your answer. Be sure to answer all the questions within a single paragraph—do not answer the questions individually.

A "paragraph" is a collection of sentences (which are not divided into separate lines) that convey a single idea throughout. The sentences in a paragraph must be logically arranged to coherently deliver your thoughts to the reader. A single paragraph must contain at least three sentences.

Question

How does Stanley's personalities change as the story continues? Why does he change that way and which characters affect him the most?

Bibliography

About the Author

Louis Sachar (68; born Mar 20, 1954) is an American author born in New York, U.S. His specialty is mystery-comedy novels for children and young adults. His most well-known works include *Holes* and the *Wayside School* series.

http://www.louissachar.com/

Other Books by the Author

Columns of each table: (from left) Title of Book; Year Published; ATOS Book Level; Lexile Measure; Interest Level.

Guide to Interest Level:
LG (Lower Grades; suitable for grades K-3)
MG (Middle Grades; suitable for grades 4-8)
MG+ (Middle Grades Plus; suitable for grades 6+)
UG (Upper Grades; suitable for grades 9-12)

Holes Series				
Holes *1999 Newbery Medal	1998	4.6	660L	MG
Stanley Yelnats' Survival Guide to Camp Green Lake	2003	4.7		MG
Small Steps	2006	4.2	690L	MG

Wayside School Series				
Sideways Stories from Wayside School	1978	3.3	460L	MG
Wayside School is Falling Down	1989	3.4	440L	MG
Wayside School Gets a Little Stranger	1995	3.3	500L	MG
Wayside School Beneath the Cloud of Doom	2020	3.9	550L	MG

Sideways Arithmetic				
Sideways Arithmetic from Wayside School	1989		670L	MG
More Sideways Arithmetic from Wayside School	1994		630L	MG

Marvin Redpost Series				
Kidnapped at Birth?	1992	2.8	520L	LG
Why Pick on Me?	1993	2.7	510L	LG
Is He a Girl?	1993	2.8	510L	LG
Alone In His Teacher's House	1994	2.9	560L	LG
Class President	1999	3.4	430L	LG
A Flying Birthday Cake?	1999	3.2	570L	LG
Super Fast, Out of Control!	2000	3.6	590L	LG
A Magic Crystal?	2000	3.1	550L	LG

Novels				
Johnny's in the Basement	1981	3.3	450L	MG
Someday Angeline	1983	4.0	610L	MG
Sixth Grade Secrets (aka Pig City in the UK)	1987	3.7	520L	MG
There's a Boy in the Girls' Bathroom	1987	3.4	490L	MG
The Boy Who Lost His Face	1989	4.0	570L	MG
Dogs Don't Tell Jokes	1991	3.8	560L	MG
The Cardturner	2010	5.0	HL720L	MG
Fuzzy Mud	2015	5.0	700L	MG

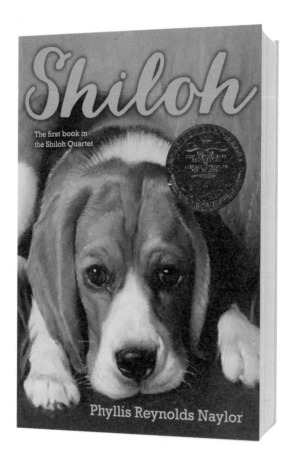

Shiloh

by Phyllis Reynolds Naylor

Published	1991 (1992 Newbery Medal)
ATOS Book Level	4.4
Lexile	890L
Word Count	29617

Plot Introduction

Have you ever met a stray dog or a cat on the streets? We all have our soft spots for homeless animals, and it's natural to want to help them. Unfortunately, it's often challenging to put that into action. Perhaps our 11-year-old protagonist, Marty Preston, is a bit braver than most of us—upon meeting a presumably stray beagle during his usual stroll around his house, he did not hesitate to take him in. Marty names the dog Shiloh and introduces him to his parents. To his surprise, Marty discovers that Shiloh is *not* actually a stray—he belongs to Judd Travers, whom Marty does not like at all. Fair enough, there are several unlikable qualities of Judd: he is typically rude to others, hunts animals out of season, frequently tells lies, and, most importantly, mistreats his dogs. Despite Judd's abusive nature (and Marty's distraught), Marty's parents logically force him to return Shiloh to his rightful owner. Thankfully, Shiloh runs away from Judd's place the next day and returns to Marty's home. This time, Marty decides to keep Shiloh for himself. He builds a makeshift pen for Shiloh and starts taking care of him: taking him for walks and giving him food from his own dinner leftovers. Then, one day, Shiloh gets attacked by the neighbor's German Shepherd and severely injured. This unfortunate event ends up revealing Marty's secret to his parents, who express their disapproval of his deception. Once again, Marty is forced to return Shiloh to Judd. But this time, Marty decides to bargain with Judd to secure Shiloh as his once and for all. Will Marty be able to make Judd an offer he can't refuse?

Themes

The scent of *justice* is pretty potent in this novel. The way Marty handles the situation regarding Shiloh showcases how the "right" action could be different from the "best" action. In Marty's case, the "right" action was to return Shiloh to his rightful owner, Judd Travers. However, Marty knows that this will inevitably lead to Shiloh's suffering. Hence the "best" action, in Marty's eyes, was to keep Shiloh away from Judd by taking care of him himself. Unfortunately, this evidently violates the law: to take custody of a dog that already has an owner is a plain theft. Thankfully, our protagonist figures out an excellent way to resolve the situation by the end of the book. Sadly, such a dilemma occurs quite frequently in real life. And often, we are compelled to pick the "right" choice to stay out of trouble. The takeaway from this book is that we should always try to devise a compromise like Marty and wisely untangle such tricky situations.

Another considerable idea from the book is *animal abuse*. Whatever the pathetic excuse is, people who mistreat animals must face severe punishment. Animals are lifeforms just like humans; under no circumstance can animal abuse be justified. Humans have no right to play God with animals' lives. Furthermore, it is crucial to realize that physical violence is not the only form of animal abuse: whether it's accidental or deliberate, failing to feed pets properly, failing to cure their illnesses in time, and performing any act that might distress them are all classified as animal abuse. As was mentioned in the book by Marty's father, a person without the capability of properly taking care of a pet must never be allowed to own a pet.

Let's take the idea of justice a bit further. Thankfully, we now have laws that judiciously prosecute culprits of animal abuse: many legislations will confiscate the ownership of pets when any sign of animal abuse is detected. However, the constitution still has loopholes that fail to deliver true justice. You've perhaps heard of the ancient Rome principle: "*dura lex, sed lex*." This Latin idiom translates to: "the law [is] harsh, but [it is] the law." Are unjust laws still laws? Consider the following saying from Martin Luther King Jr. as well: "One has not only a legal but moral responsibility to obey just laws. Conversely, one has a moral responsibility to disobey unjust laws." What do you think we should do with unjust laws? And how do you think we can prevent unjust laws from being implemented?

Another minor idea from the book relates to *telling lies*. Perhaps you've heard of "white lies." They refer to lies told with good intentions (like how you tell your friend that their hair looks great even after their hairdresser messed it up). However, similar to several other ideas in the book, these "white lies" also feel subjective. A white lie for you may be worse for someone else; your "good intention" may not be so "good" for others. What's your position on telling lies, especially white lies?

1 Summary and First Impressions

A. Can you give a short summary of the story?

B. What do you think about the story? Do you like it?

C. If you were Marty, would you have kept Shiloh to yourself? Why or why not?

2 Story Questions

A. When Marty first encounters Shiloh, why does he think the dog might have been abused?

B. Why is Marty unsure about keeping Shiloh? Why does his parents not let him keep Shiloh?

C. Why does Marty not like Judd? Can you name all the reasons why Marty doesn't like Judd?

D. When Shiloh returned to Marty's home after running away from Judd again, what did Marty do? Why did he do that?

E. Why does Marty feel bad about himself as he protects Shiloh? What does he constantly do to keep Shiloh a secret from his friends and family?

F. How does Marty's mother find out that Marty is keeping Shiloh to himself? How does she know that Marty is keeping a secret?

G. What happens to Shiloh the night Marty's mother finds out about him? What does Marty's father do when he saw what happened?

H. What does Marty decide to do to keep Shiloh? How does he bargain with Judd? What was Judd's answer and what was their final deal?

I. What does Marty learn about Judd (especially about his childhood) as he works for him? How does Judd's thoughts about Marty change during this process?

    A. How is Marty like toward his parents? Does he respect them?

    B. Is Marty responsible? Think about the time Shiloh first arrived at Marty's home. Also, think about what Marty did to take Shiloh away from Judd.

    C. Does Marty love animals? How does he feel about animals?

    D. How does Marty feel about telling lies? Is he comfortable, or does he feel guilty about it?

    E. How does Marty feel about laws that don't protect animals from abuse? How is Marty's understanding with justice?

    F. What is Judd like? What are his characteristics?

    G. Why is Judd the way he is? How and why does Judd change as Marty works for him?

④ Theme Questions

    A. Marty continuously told lies in order to keep Shiloh a secret. However, perhaps his intentions were pure—to save Shiloh's life.
       Do you approve of Marty telling lies to protect Shiloh? Do you think it's okay to tell lies if it's to do what you think is right? If not, what do you think Marty should have done instead (when Shiloh returned to his home)?

    B. In the book, Marty's parents state that Judd has the right to keep Shiloh in his custody even if he mistreats him, as he is the rightful owner of the dog.
       What do you think about this law—is it fair? What do you think about unfair laws? Do you know any examples of unfair laws? Should everyone still obey unfair laws?

Vocabulary Exercise

Instructions

These are some words and phrases used in *Shiloh*. Write each of their definition in English. Then, for each word, create your own sentence including that word. Be mindful that one word can have multiple meanings or be used in more than one way. Carefully consider how the words and phrases were used in the original book, and try to use each word/phrase the same way as how the book used it.

Words & Phrases

abandon	commence	decency	enthusiastic	envy
investigate	mournful	suspicious	sympathetic	omit

Sentences from the book

Here are the sentences from the original book that contains the given words and phrases. Only use these as reference and do not write the same sentences for your exercise.

abandon: Dad's crossing the bridge by the old **abandoned** gristmill, turning at the boarded-up school.

commence: … and then he **commences** to slobber love all over me as well.

decency: "Somebody knows my dog is missing, takes him in, and don't even have the **decency** to tell me?"

enthusiasm: I ask David, trying to dig up the least little bit of **enthusiasm.**

envy: First time I ever saw any **envy** in my Ma.

investigate: Tyler County hasn't hardly got the money to **investigate** reports of children being kicked, Dad says, much less dogs.

mournful: … putting his nose in everyone's lap, looking **mournful**, waiting for somebody to slip him something to eat.

suspicious. … but if he's already **suspicious** about me, that'll only make it worse.

sympathetic: … making low **sympathy** noises in her throat, the way she does when Dara Lynn or Becky or me gets sick.

omit: If I tell Ma and Dad everything except about the deer, that's lying by **omission** …

Paragraph Write-up Exercise

Instructions

Write a short paragraph expressing your thoughts about the following questions. There are multiple questions to guide you arrange your thoughts and form your answer. Be sure to answer all the questions within a single paragraph—do not answer the questions individually.

A "paragraph" is a collection of sentences (which are not divided into separate lines) that convey a single idea throughout. The sentences in a paragraph must be logically arranged to coherently deliver your thoughts to the reader. A single paragraph must contain at least three sentences.

Question

How do you feel about Marty's behaviors as he was trying to keep Shiloh a secret (especially him telling lies)? What would you have done if you were Marty?

Bibliography

About the Author

Phyllis Reynolds Naylor (89; born Jan 4, 1933) is an American author born in Indiana, U.S. Her specialty is heartwarming, slice-of-life novels for children and young adults. Her most well-known works include *Shiloh* and the *Alice* series.

http://phyllisnaylor.com/

Other Books by the Author

Columns of each table: (from left) Title of Book; Year Published; ATOS Book Level; Lexile Measure; Interest Level.

Guide to Interest Level:

LG (Lower Grades; suitable for grades K-3)

MG (Middle Grades; suitable for grades 4-8)

MG+ (Middle Grades Plus; suitable for grades 6+)

UG (Upper Grades; suitable for grades 9-12)

Shiloh Series				
Shiloh *1992 Newbery Medal	1991	4.4	890L	MG
Shiloh Season	1996	4.8	860L	MG
Saving Shiloh	1997	4.9	1020L	MG
A Shiloh Christmas	2015	5.0	940L	MG

The Alice Collection: Alice in Elementary				
Starting With Alice	2002	4.6	730L	MG
Alice in Blunderland	2003	4.2	700L	MG
Lovingly Alice	2004	4.3	710L	MG

The Alice Collection: The Middle School Years				
The Agony of Alice	1985	5.3	910L	MG
Alice in Rapture, Sort of	1989	4.9	840L	UG
Reluctantly Alice	1991	5.0	860L	UG
All but Alice	1992	5.0	810L	UG
Alice in April	1993	4.5	710L	UG
Alice in-Between	1994	5.0	780L	UG
Alice the Brave	1995	5.1	820L	UG
Alice in Lace	1996	4.8	800L	UG
Outrageously Alice	1997	5.0	740L	UG
Achingly Alice	1998	4.9	750L	UG
Alice on the Outside	1999	4.9	780L	UG
The Grooming of Alice	2000	4.9	740L	UG

** For the older audience: The Alice Collection: High School and Beyond (17 Books)

Number the Stars

by Lois Lowry

Published	1989 (1990 Newbery Medal)
ATOS Book Level	4.5
Lexile	670L
Word Count	27197

Plot Introduction

History, despite its wrenching pain, cannot be unlived; but if faced with courage, need not be lived again. – Maya Angelou

Sorry folks, this book is nothing to joke about. This book handles the "Holocaust"—the mass murder of almost six million innocent European Jews by the German Nazis throughout World War II (WWII). Allow me to set the scene first: the place is Copenhagen, Denmark, and the year is 1943. Three years have passed since the Nazi forces took over Denmark. Our heroine is Annemarie Johansen, a resolute non-Jewish 10-year-old girl with a Jewish friend, Ellen Rosen. Annemarie has recently been noticing some unpleasant changes around her—she once encountered Nazi soldiers on her way to school, and she noticed that her Jewish neighbor closed their store. Ellen's family has caught these changes too, and they decide they must leave Copenhagen immediately. However, they gather that leaving altogether may be risky and decide to leave Ellen under Johansens' custody for a day. While her parents safely make their escape, Ellen has a heart-shaking encounter with the Nazi soldiers who storm into Annemarie's house, looking for her and her parents. Thankfully, Mr. Johansen manages to fool the soldiers and keeps Ellen's identity hidden. The next day, Mrs. Johansen takes Annemarie, Ellen, and Kirstie (Annemarie's little sister) to Uncle Henrik's. Disguised as an ordinary fisherman, Henrik smuggles Jewish people to the nearby Swedish shore—where the Nazi force is absent—by hiding them inside his boat. During the covert evacuation process, Mrs. Johansen gets injured and fails to deliver a crucial package to Henrik. Now, Annemarie must deliver the package, confronting the Nazi soldiers on her own. Will she successfully save the countless lives of Jewish people, including her friend, Ellen?

Themes

While not necessarily a "theme," the historical background of this book is certainly worth discussing. Before you read this part, here's a disclaimer: what follows is a considerably simplified summary of the actual event; it is devoid of *numerous* critical details, and I advise you to search and study this history yourself. The horrific genocide of European Jews—often referred to as the "Holocaust"—occurred throughout WWII, between 1941 and

1945. This unlawful "ethnic cleansing" resulted in the tragic deaths of roughly *six million* Jews (almost 2/3 of the entire European Jewish population at the time!). Merciless German Nazis, led by the maleficent Adolf Hitler, put helpless innocent Jews in concentration camps—the most widely-known one being Auschwitz—where they were tortured and murdered. The major motif for this incident was anti-Semitism, a form of racism against Jews. While anti-Semitism emerged from religious bases (the Jews' refusal to accept and acknowledge other religions), anti-Semitism in Germany is also attributed to the rumor that the Jews were to blame for the country's defeat in World War I (WWI). This horrific genocide concluded in 1945 with Germany's loss in WWII and Adolf Hitler's suicide.

Returning to the story, we must discuss several themes regarding our heroine, Annemarie. Perhaps the most conspicuous theme is *growing up*. Becoming mature may be a beautiful thing from afar, but it's not always exciting to receive the spotlight. The process is overflowing with confusion and heartache. And a war going on in the background doesn't help at all. As Annemarie experiences throughout the novel, one of the key aspects of growing up is shaping your own identity. During the process, you inevitably have to move on from the world of children to the world of adults. While this dilemma usually doesn't arrive until one's final teenage years, war forces Annemarie to experience it much earlier than usual. She may still have the body of a child, but she is forced to carry the responsibilities of an adult (such as protecting her loved ones and showing bravery in danger). What's worse is that the adults think she's still too young for all this, and no one explains the precise situation to her. The death of her older sister, the disappearance of the Jews, the job of Uncle Henrik—all these are left for Annemarie to decipher herself. As an outlook, here's some food for thought: will you be able to mature as fast as Annemarie if you were her?

Other minor themes include *bravery* and *knowledge*. It's apparent that Annmarie grew a pair in front of the Nazi soldiers—in fact, she gets better with every encounter throughout the book. What's easy to overlook is her *strategy* (i.e., *how* she could act bravely in front of them), which especially shines during the final encounter while she delivers the handkerchief. The book states that she takes inspiration from her mother's words, "act like a little girl who doesn't know anything," and how her little sister, Kirstie, acted in front of the soldiers during the train ride to Gilleleje. Perhaps ignorance and bravery aren't all that different. This leads to the second minor theme: as stated above, Annemarie misses out on lots of details related to the war due to the adults thinking that she's not old enough. However, you could also say that ignorance *allows* her to be braver. Sometimes, not knowing everything may infuse you with courage.

Questions

1 Summary and First Impressions

    A. Can you give a short summary of the story?

    B. What do you think about the story? Do you like it?

    C. Do you think you could have been as brave in front of the Nazi soldiers as Annemarie?

2 Story Questions

    A. Why did the Rosens run away? How did they know the Nazis were coming for them?

    B. When the Nazis came into Annemarie's house, how did Mr. Johansen introduce Ellen? Why did the Nazis get suspicious about Ellen's identity, and how did Mr. Johansen convince them?

    C. Where did Mrs. Johansen take Annemarie, Kirstie, and Ellen to the next day? Why did they go there? Who is Uncle Henrik, and what does he do?

    D. What happened during the train ride to Uncle Henrik's? How did Kirstie act toward the soldiers? What did Annemarie think about her sister's actions?

    E. What did Uncle Henrik tell Annemarie when she asked about the big gathering? Why did she doubt Uncle Henrik's words?

    F. What did Uncle Henrik tell Annemarie when she questioned about him and his sister lying to her?

    G. What did the Nazis say when they saw the casket closed during the gathering? What did Mrs. Johansen tell them, and how were they able to keep it closed?

    H. What happens to Mrs. Johansen as she leads the Rosens toward Henrik's boat? What does she tell Annemarie to do after her daughter finds her injured?

    I. What happens to Annemarie while she is delivering the envelop to Uncle Henrik? How did she act when she encountered the soldiers?

J. What was in the envelop, and how did it help Uncle Henrik?

K. What does Uncle Henrik tell Annemarie about bravery that night?

L. What happens to the Rosens? What happens to Peter, and what does Annemarie learn about her sister, Lise's death? What does Annemarie do with Ellen's Star of David necklace?

③ Character Questions

A. Would you say Annemarie is smart? Would you say she is good at "reading between the lines"?

B. What do you think about Annemarie's ability to think and act fast in the case of an emergency? Think of how she interacted with the Nazi soldiers throughout the book.

C. Would you say Annemarie is a brave person? Would you say she understood Uncle Henrik's lessons about bravery?

D. How does Annemarie's personalities change throughout the story? Would you say she matures throughout the story?

④ Theme Questions

A. Protecting someone else and fighting for others' lives are usually responsibilities that are *not* forced upon young children like Annemarie. However, the war imposes such duties on Annemarie—she is tasked with keeping her Jewish friend, Ellen, safe.
Do you think war forces you to grow up faster and act like an adult? Do you think war would force you to bear some of the responsibilities of an adult?

B. Annemarie displays incredible bravery time and time again throughout the book. Do you think, like her, anyone can act brave when called upon? What's your thoughts on Uncle Henrik's statement: "It's much easier to be brave if you don't know everything"?

Vocabulary Exercise

These are some words and phrases used in *Number the Stars*. Write each of their definition in English. Then, for each word, create your own sentence including that word. Be mindful that one word can have multiple meanings or be used in more than one way. Carefully consider how the words and phrases were used in the original book, and try to use each word/phrase the same way as how the book used it.

Words & Phrases

curfew	hesitate	congregation	frightened	reluctantly
timid	puzzled	affectionately	fascinated	dismayed

Sentences from the book

Here are the sentences from the original book that contains the given words and phrases. Only use these as reference and do not write the same sentences for your exercise.

curfew: Copenhagen had a **curfew**, and no citizens were allowed out after eight o'clock.

hesitated: Then she **hesitated** and glanced at her mother, fearful that she had said the wrong thing …

congregation: This morning, at the synagogue, the rabbi told his **congregation** that the Nazis have taken the synagogue lists of all the Jews.

frightened: Ellen had said that her mother was **frightened** of the ocean, that it was too cold and too big.

reluctantly: Kirstie had gone to bed **reluctantly**, complaining that she wanted to stay up …

timid: … who gave a lazy, rough-textured lick to the palm of Ellen's hand when she extended it **timidly**.

puzzled: She could see, too, that Mr. Rosen had a **puzzled** look. He didn't know what the packet contained.

affectionately: He rubbed the cow's neck **affectionately**.

fascinated: She had always been **fascinated** by her mother's stories of her own childhood.

dismayed: She was startled. And **dismayed**. It was a question she did not want to be asked.

Paragraph Write-up Exercise

Instructions

Write a short paragraph expressing your thoughts about the following questions. There are multiple questions to guide you arrange your thoughts and form your answer. Be sure to answer all the questions within a single paragraph—do not answer the questions individually.

A "paragraph" is a collection of sentences (which are not divided into separate lines) that convey a single idea throughout. The sentences in a paragraph must be logically arranged to coherently deliver your thoughts to the reader. A single paragraph must contain at least three sentences.

Question

Would your childhood being a war time make the process of you growing up more complicated? Why would, or why would it not be more complicated compared to growing up under normal conditions?

Bibliography

1 – "The Holocaust" from *History.com* (https://www.history.com/topics/world-war-ii/the-holocaust)

2 – "Holocaust" from *Encyclopedia Britannica* (https://www.britannica.com/event/Holocaust)

About the Author

Lois Lowry (85; born Mar 20, 1937) is an American children and young-adult author born in Hawaii, U.S. She specializes in weaving complex subject matters into her stories. She is also known for her writings about dystopias. Her most well-known works include *The Giver* series, *Number the Stars*, and *Rabble Starkey*.

https://loislowry.com/

Other Books by the Author

Columns of each table: (from left) Title of Book; Year Published; ATOS Book Level; Lexile Measure; Interest Level.

Guide to Interest Level:

LG (Lower Grades; suitable for grades K-3)

MG (Middle Grades; suitable for grades 4-8)

MG+ (Middle Grades Plus; suitable for grades 6+)

UG (Upper Grades; suitable for grades 9-12)

Giver Series				
The Giver *1994 Newbery Medal	1993	5.7	760L	MG
Gathering Blue	2000	5.0	680L	MG+
Messenger	2004	4.9	720L	MG+
Son	2012	5.0	720L	MG+

Sam Krupnik Series				
All About Sam	1988	4.0	670L	MG
Attaboy, Sam	1992	4.6	740L	MG
See You Around, Sam!	1996	4.4	740L	MG
Zooman Sam	1999	4.1	680L	MG

Just the Tates! Series

The One Hundredth Thing About Caroline	1983	4.6	690L	MG
Switcharound	1985	4.6	680L	MG
Your Move, J.P.!	1990	4.9	750L	MG

Willoughbys Series

The Willoughbys	2008	5.2	790L	MG
The Willoughbys Return	2020	4.8		MG

Anastasia Krupnik Series

Anastasia Krupnik	1979	4.5	700L	MG
Anastasia Again!	1981	4.5	700L	MG
Anastasia at Your Service	1982	4.3	670L	MG
Anastasia, Ask Your Analyst	1984	4.2	630L	MG
Anastasia on Her Own	1985	4.4	640L	MG
Anastasia Has the Answers	1986	4.9	760L	MG
Anastasia's Chosen Career	1987	4.5	730L	MG
Anastasia at This Address	1991	4.6	730L	MG
Anastasia, Absolutely	1995	4.7	780L	MG

Novels

A Summer to Die	1977	5.3	800L	UG
Find A Stranger, Say Goodbye	1978	4.8	780L	UG
Autumn Street	1980	5.1	810L	MG
Taking Care of Terrific	1983	5.3	840L	MG
Rabble Starkey	1987	5.3	940L	MG
Number the Stars *1990 Newbery Medal	1989	4.5	670L	MG
Stay! Keeper's Story	1997	6.4	880L	MG
The Silent Boy	2003	5.1	870L	MG
Gossamer	2006	4.4	660L	MG
Crow Call (picture books)	2009	3.8	AD750L	LG
The Birthday Ball	2010	5.2	810L	MG
Bless this Mouse	2011	4.5	690L	LG

Nonfiction				
Looking Back: A Book of Memories	1998	5.5	900L	MG
On the Horizon: World War II Reflections	2020	4.2	HL580L	MG

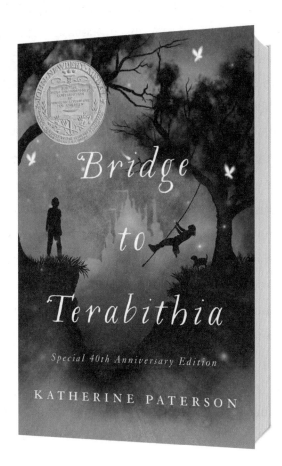

Bridge to Terabithia

by Katherine Paterson

Published	1977 (1978 Newbery Medal)
ATOS Book Level	4.6
Lexile	810L
Word Count	32888

Plot Introduction

The Newbery Award sure has a preference toward books about puberty. Of its various enchanting aspects, this book explores the process of discovering who you truly are. Our main character, Jess Aarons, is an insecure eleven-year-old boy who shares his house with *five* sisters. Being the only boy in the house, it's not easy for him to get his father's attention and approval, which he dreads. His father wants Jess to "act like a man," and Jess tries his best to fulfill his father's expectations. But there's one problem: Jess's favorite activity is *to draw*—a pastime his father considers "sissy." Hence, Jess practices *running*—he thinks that if he could win the race at school, then his father would surely be impressed. Uh oh, *here comes a new challenger!* Just when Jess thought he had the race in the bag, Leslie, a female transfer student, rises triumphant against all the other male contestants, including Jess. While Jess is dismayed at first, this loss turns out to be the start of an amazing friendship. Soon, Jess and Leslie realize they share something extraordinary: *creativity*. Through this, they create their own imaginary country called "Terabithia" in the woods. The two grow close as friends as they spend time together in Terabithia. Leslie uncovers her true character as the "cool girl" who doesn't care about how others perceive her. As Jess spends more time with her, his personality also gets shaped to be more confident and resilient. Leslie also enthusiastically supports Jess's artistic explorations—a first for Jess. Unfortunately, the day arrives when Leslie can no longer accompany Jess. Shall Jess carry on and finish his transformation without his dearest friend?

Themes

Growing up is a magical thing, and at the center of it, there is *discovering who you truly are*. *Bridge to Terabithia* probes two essential elements of growing up: 1) *the role of friendship* and 2) *gender*.

First, let's talk about *friendship*. Friendship is not only the most important relationship in this book, but it often is so in real life as well. There are certain aids that only your friends can provide, and there are certain matters that you can only disclose to your friends. Sometimes, you might even feel closer to your friends than your family. The most notable friendship in this story is (obviously) that between Jess and Leslie. Let's break it down from Jess's point of view first. Barely anyone around Jess—his family members, friends, and school teachers—understands and appreciates his creativity and passion for art. However, Leslie acknowledges these qualities and supports Jess to prosper. Without proper support, great talents can easily collapse; on the other hand, even a single fan can spark miracles. Now, onto Leslie's point of view. Throughout the story, we learn that Leslie's parents are both extremely busy, and they barely have time for their own daughter. Thankfully, Leslie could find refuge in her friendship with Jess, who has all the time to pay attention to her. The friendship provided her the comfort and love she had never experienced before. While this friendship is clearly a win-win situation, an interesting question arises: is this friendship truly *equal*? Did Leslie and Jess share the same amount of love and help for each other? How about in real life—is every friendship *equivalent*? *Should* it be equivalent? Is it okay if it's not?

Next up: *gender*. Gender conflict is one of the main drives of the story. In short (though I consider these expressions inappropriate), Jess is a "girlish" boy, while Leslie is a "boyish" girl. Jess loves art and daydreaming, but he is insecure about these qualities. He's also generally timid in social interactions, especially at the beginning of the book. Conversely, Leslie upholds a confident attitude, and she loves sports. Their personalities and hobbies flag them as "different" and isolate them from the rest of the school kids. However, there's *nothing wrong* with either of them. In fact, no activity or personality trait should be labeled "boyish" or "girlish." A related issue here is *fitting in*. As mentioned, there's nothing wrong with being distinguished; you don't have to exhaust yourself trying to be like others—it only makes you *less you*. Be yourself, and don't be afraid to show it.

A minor addendum to *growing up*: I'd like you to reconsider the end of the book. (*Spoiler ahead*) A tragic event near the end of the story left Jess deeply depressed. But he did not let it completely break him; he soon found the strength to carry on. How was this possible? Would it have been possible if he still had his personality at the start of the book? If not, how did his personality change, and why?

Questions

① Summary and First Impressions

A. Can you give a short summary of the story?

B. What do you think about the story? Do you like it?

C. Have you ever had a friend as inspiring/influential as Leslie? How would you feel if you lost that friend through an accident?

② Story Questions

A. Why is Jess obsessed with running? Why does he want to win the race at school so badly?

B. What is Jess's actual hobby? What do his family and school friends think about this activity? Why does Jess not dare show is dad his drawings?

C. Why does Jess like Miss Edmunds? What did she say after she saw one of Jess's paintings? How did Jess feel about her comments?

D. Why was Jess not pleased with Leslie arriving at school *at first*? Which events led the two to become friends?

E. When Jess and Leslie first visited the creek in the woods, what did Leslie suggest to make? Why did she want to make their own country in the woods?

F. What activities do Jess and Leslie do together in Terabithia?

G. What do Jess's parents think about Leslie and Jess always hanging out with each other? Do they like it or not?

H. Where do Jess and Miss Edmunds go to together? What happens to Leslie while Jess is away?

I. What does Jess do as a final act for Terabithia and Leslie?

J. Why does Jess feel the need to move forward, leaving Terabithia behind? How does he describe Terabithia toward the end of the story?

A. At the start of the story, how is Jess like, especially in his confidence and self-esteem?

B. What does Jess's peers and parents think about him drawing? Is he sensitive about these comments?

C. How does Jess's father want him to act like? How does Jess feel about this?

D. Why does Jess feel the need to be the fastest runner in fifth grade? Why does he think this would impress his peers and (especially) his father?

E. Does Jess feel like he belongs to his community/family? Does he feel like a unique and special member of his community/family?

F. Is Jess creative and imaginative? What kind of things does he draw?

G. Is Jess sensitive and sympathetic? Recall what he thought when Leslie admitted that her house doesn't have a TV in front of the class.

H. How does Jess change as Leslie comes along?

I. How was Jess able to carry on with his new self even after losing Leslie?

④ Theme Questions

A. Both Jess and Leslie benefit incredibly from their friendship. Namely, Jess grew a thick skin and became less sensitive toward the negative comments about him by closely observing Leslie's confident demeanor. On the other hand, Leslie receives the love and care she never (but should have) received from her busy parents.

Like them, do you think friendship in real life is always mutual? Do you think friends always exchange equal amounts of love, care, and support? And, even if the friends gain different types of aid, can they ultimately amount to be the same?

B. Throughout the story, both Leslie and Jess suffer from being different from the stereotypical "girl" and "boy," respectively. Unlike other girls, Leslie has short hair, wears pants, enjoys sports, and is quite confident. And, unlike other boys, Jess is shy and self-conscious, loves to draw, and doesn't have a particular liking toward sports. Throughout the story, thankfully, Jess and Leslie were able to find comfort in each other's company.

Do you think there are certain roles fit for each gender? Do you think each gender should try to keep certain characteristics/features expected for them?

Vocabulary Exercise

Instructions

These are some words and phrases used in *Bridge to Terabithia*. Write each of their definition in English. Then, for each word, create your own sentence including that word. Be mindful that one word can have multiple meanings or be used in more than one way. Carefully consider how the words and phrases were used in the original book, and try to use each word/phrase the same way as how the book used it.

Words & Phrases

complacent	discourage	talented	genuine	delighted
conspicuous	deliberately	dare	quivering	ridiculous

Sentences from the book

Here are the sentences from the original book that contains the given words and phrases. Only use these as reference and do not write the same sentences for your exercise.

complacent: Jess was glad to escape the shed and the **complacent** company of Miss Bessie.

talented & discourage: She said he was "unusually **talented**," and she hoped he wouldn't let anything **discourage** him, but would "keep it up."

genuine: "Why?" It was a **genuine** question. Leslie wasn't being smarty.

delighted: "Daddy!" May Belle screamed with **delight** and started running for the road.

conspicuous: … while the smaller boys tried to include themselves without being **conspicuous**.

deliberately: He felt there in the teachers' room that it was the beginning of a new season in his life, and he chose **deliberately** to make it so.

dare: They didn't dare **build** a fire in the castle.

quivering: He wasn't sure, he thought her voice was **quivering**, but he wasn't going to start feeling sorry for her again.

ridiculous: It was the most **ridiculous** thing he had never heard.

Paragraph Write-up Exercise

Instructions

Write a short paragraph expressing your thoughts about the following questions. There are multiple questions to guide you arrange your thoughts and form your answer. Be sure to answer all the questions within a single paragraph—do not answer the questions individually.

A "paragraph" is a collection of sentences (which are not divided into separate lines) that convey a single idea throughout. The sentences in a paragraph must be logically arranged to coherently deliver your thoughts to the reader. A single paragraph must contain at least three sentences.

Question

Which characteristics do Jess and Leslie share? How are they so compatible? How would the story have gone if their personalities were reversed?

Bibliography

Katherine Womeldorf Paterson (89; born Oct 31, 1932) is an American children and young-adults' author born in Jiangsu, Republic of China. She specializes in handling mature topics such as death and envy. She often writes about protagonists who go through hardship followed by triumph. Her most well-known works include *Bridge to Terabithia*, *The Great Gilly Hopkins*, and *Jacob Have I Loved*.

https://katherinepaterson.com/

Other Books by the Author

Columns of each table: (from left) Title of Book; Year Published; ATOS Book Level; Lexile Measure; Interest Level.

Guide to Interest Level:
LG (Lower Grades; suitable for grades K-3)
MG (Middle Grades; suitable for grades 4-8)
MG+ (Middle Grades Plus; suitable for grades 6+)
UG (Upper Grades; suitable for grades 9-12)

Novels				
The Master Puppeteer	1975	5.4	860L	MG
Bridge to Terabithia *1978 Newbery Medal	1977	4.6	810L	MG
The Great Gilly Hopkins * 1979 Newbery Honor	1978	4.6	800L	MG
Jacob Have I Loved *1981 Newbery Medal	1980	5.7	880L	MG
Rebels of the Heavenly Kingdom	1983	6.0	890L	UG
Come Sing Jimmy Jo	1985	4.7	760L	MG
Park's Quest	1988	4.2	710L	MG
Lyddie	1991	5.6	860L	MG
The King's Equal	1992	5.2	780L	LG

Flip-Flop Girl	1994	4.6	720L	MG
Jip, His Story	1996	5.3	860L	MG
Preacher's Boy	1999	5.2	860L	MG
The Same Stuff as Stars	2002	4.3	670L	MG
Bread and Roses, Too	2006	4.9	810	MG
The Day of the Pelican	2009	5.2	770L	MG
My Brigadista Year	2017	5.3	830L	MG
Birdie's Bargain	2021			

Flip-Flop Girl 1994 4.6 720L MG

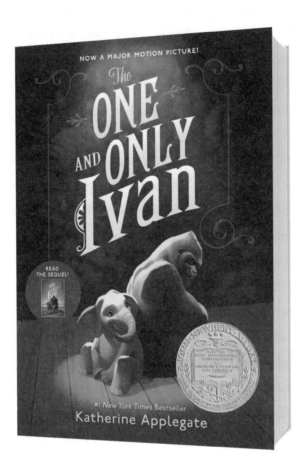

The One and Only Ivan

by Katherine Applegate

Published	2012 (2013 Newbery Medal)
ATOS Book Level	3.6
Lexile	570L
Word Count	26263

Plot Introduction

Did you know that placing wild animals in cages can provoke intense stress? When wild animals are not provided sufficient space to roam, their mental health deteriorates, causing them to walk in circles or even harm themselves. Sadly, our hero today, Ivan, is a silverback gorilla who lives in a compact glass-walled "domain" inside a shopping mall owned by a person called Mack. Ivan was born in Central Africa; while he was still a baby, he was captured by humans. Ivan then traveled all the way to the United States, where he was adopted by Mack. Ivan was raised in Mack's house until he grew too big and was moved to his current domain; he has stayed there for over twenty-seven years. Thankfully, he made some friends: Stella, a former circus elephant with an injured foot, lives right next to Ivan, and Bob, a stray dog, slipped through a crack in Ivan's cage and made it his new home. Stella and Bob educate Ivan about the outside world and tells him how *great* of a place a zoo is. Unfortunately, Mack doesn't treat his animals as well as a zoo does—he forces Stella and Ivan to perform circus three times a day and uses violence if they do not obey. One day, a baby elephant named Ruby arrives newly at the mall. Placed in the same cage as Stella, Ruby receives excellent nurturing from her. Unfortunately, Stella's foot infection keeps getting worse, and she ends up passing away. The night before she leaves, she makes Ivan promise that he will ensure Ruby a better life than what she had lived. Remembering Stella's praises about zoos, Ivan decides he must send Ruby to a zoo. Will Ivan keep his promise and save Ruby's life?

Themes

The striking theme of *The One and Only Ivan* is *animal rights*. Ivan, Stella, and Ruby remain trapped in tiny, confined spaces for almost the entire book. Moreover, we constantly encounter cases of indisputable animal mistreatment: Stella mentions that circus animals are often chained to one spot for prolonged times to "break their spirit;" we also witness Mack using violence to train Ruby for tricks. Experts assert that, on top of inflicting violence, keeping wild animals in captivity *per se* can also induce extreme stress. This begs an interesting question: *Does the book conclude with a genuinely happy ending for Ivan and Ruby?* Admittedly, after relocating to the zoo, they obtained larger cages, friendship (i.e., more of their respective kinds), and better care. But ultimately, they're still locked up in cages. Is that the best outcome for the two? Conversely, had they been directly released to the wild from the shopping mall, would they have been able to survive? With them staying under human care for extended times, they likely have forgotten "the ways of the wild"—their natural instincts must have deteriorated. What do you think? What would be the best ending for Ivan and Ruby? Do you think they found true happiness at the zoo?

Let's now cover some minor themes. First, the book touches on the effects of *isolation*. Living away from his own kind took a hard toll on Ivan—he has forgotten most of "the ways of a silverback." This registers when he eventually reunites with other silverbacks at the zoo. Even by the end of the book, Ivan isn't sure if he belongs in the primate circle. Next, the book also handles *the power of art*. In the book, Ivan ultimately saves Ruby by expressing himself through art. His masterpiece, which shows Ruby inside a zoo cage and features the word "home" below, clearly addresses his argument that Ruby belongs in a zoo. Albeit with some confusion, Julia, George, and all the animal activists eventually figure out the true meaning of his ingenuity. Through this, perhaps the author is trying to convey how expressive a piece of art could be. After all, *a picture is worth a thousand words*.

As a side note, our hero Ivan is based on a real silverback gorilla of the same name. Ivan was born in the Democratic Republic of Congo and lived with his parents and twin sister. While he was still an infant, he and his twin sister got captured by humans and brought to the US, during which process his twin sister unfortunately died. In the US, Ivan was adopted by a local corner store owner and raised like a human baby in his home. Soon, however, he grew too big and was relocated to a circus-themed mall in Washington state. It is said that there were other exotic animals in captivity at the mall then, but it's not sure if there were any elephants (like Stella and Ruby). Ivan lived in the mall for *twenty-seven years*; during this time, he had to endure the everlastingly increasing loneliness and discomfort. Near the end of his stay, a National Geographic documentary about him, *The Urban Gorilla*, aired, and the calls for Ivan's freedom broke out across the country. Soon after, the mall went bankrupt, and Ivan moved to Zoo Atlanta. Ivan lived his later life in the loving care of the zookeepers, enjoying his fame. And, just like in the book, Ivan loved to paint! His paintings were sold at Zoo Atlanta as souvenirs. In 2012, Ivan passed away at 50—a very good age for a silverback—leaving no offspring. Ivan's story is readily available online—if you're interested, have a go!

Questions

① Summary and First Impressions

A. Can you give a short summary of the story?

B. What do you think about the story? Do you like it?

C. What are your thoughts on people who keep animals in captivity for their own profit?

② Story Questions

A. Where does Ivan live? What does he do there every day?

B. How did Ivan arrive at the mall? (Where was he born, what kind of life did he live, and what events happened before he came to the mall?)

C. Who is Stella, the elephant? What does she do at the mall? How did Stella arrive at the mall?

D. Who is Bob, the dog? What does he do at the mall? How did Bob arrive at the mall?

E. What objects did Julia give Ivan through the crack in his cage? What did Ivan do with those items?

F. How does Stella describe zoos to Ivan?

G. What animal arrives newly at the mall? What is its name and how did it come to the mall?

H. What does Stella make Ivan promise before she dies?

I. What does Ivan paint to save Ruby? What word does he write in his painting? How does he know what that word means?

J. Who does Ivan show his drawing to and what do they do with it?

K. After Ivan's painting is put on the billboard, a lot of people come to the mall. Who are they and what are they doing there?

L. Where do Ivan and Ruby move to at the end of the story? What happens to Bob, Julia, and George, respectively?

③ Character Questions

A. How does Ivan describe humans? What does he think about humans talking? What does he think about how humans treat animals?

B. Do you think Ivan is curious? Does he question a lot? Is he clever and observant?

C. Does Ivan experience a sort of identity crisis throughout the story? Does he question where he belongs (to humans or to silverbacks)?

D. Is Ivan bad at remembering? Or is he good at remembering but doesn't want to remember?

E. Does Ivan adapt to his environment well? How did he react when he was first captured? How did he react after meeting the other silverbacks at the zoo for the first time?

F. Is Ivan kind and warm-hearted? Does he care for his friends and their health? How does he treat his friends?

G. How does Stella describe the way people treat animals at a circus to teach them tricks? Why was she worried when Ruby first arrived at the mall?

H. How does Bob feel about humans at first? How does he change?

④ Theme Questions

A. Let's think about the ending for a bit. The book paints it as a happy ending: after moving to the zoo, Ivan and Ruby acquired more space (i.e., bigger cages), company (i.e., more of their respective species), and better care (by the zookeepers). However, the zoo still keeps their animals, including Ivan and Ruby, in cages. Admittedly, the conditions are a lot better than the mall—zookeepers constantly give sufficient food, clean their cages, and look out for their health. Still, the zoo confines Ivan and Ruby to limited domains and offers them only restricted activities.

Do you think Ivan and Ruby found true happiness at the zoo? Do you think they would have wanted to return to the wild instead? Do you think they could survive in the wild if they were set free?

B. Growing up with humans and being away from silverbacks for so long, Ivan undergoes a major identity crisis on whether he belongs to the world of humans or that of silverbacks. He also displays timid and uncomfortable behaviors when he mixes in with the other silverbacks at the zoo for the first time.

Do you think one's childhood environment builds the person's identity more than their instincts or inheritance? Had Ivan been allowed to grow up like a human (instead of moving to the mall), do you think he would have been able to understand human language and act like a human?

C. Since Ivan is telling the tale in this book, its language is slightly broken. The book omits basic grammar components and intentionally uses incorrect grammar to reimagine Ivan's speech.

What do you think about the language of this book? Does it fit Ivan? Do you think it's okay for books to break the rules to fit its interests?

Vocabulary Exercise

These are some words and phrases used in *The One and Only Ivan*. Write each of their definition in English. Then, for each word, create your own sentence including that word. Be mindful that one word can have multiple meanings or be used in more than one way. Carefully consider how the words and phrases were used in the original book, and try to use each word/phrase the same way as how the book used it.

Words & Phrases

domain	venture	precious	frantically	opportunity
patient	tolerant	recognize	make amends	conveniently

Sentences from the book

Here are the sentences from the original book that contains the given words and phrases. Only use these as reference and do not write the same sentences for your exercise.

domain: My **domain** is at one end of the ring. I live here …

venture: Slowly, carefully, a young gorilla begins to **venture** farther and farther away

precious: "Memories are **precious**," Stella adds. "They help tell us who we are."

frantically: They hunt **frantically**, stalking, pushing, grumbling.

opportunity: Once I asked Stella if she'd ever had any babies. / She shook her head. "I never had the **opportunity**."

patient: Bob opened one eye. "Be **patient**." / "I'm tired of being **patient**," I say.

tolerant: Then I would join her and we would bounce on that **tolerant** belly until he gave us the Grunt …

recognize: Humans don't always seem to **recognize** what I've drawn.

The One and Only Ivan **71**

make amends: "It has room to roam and humans who don't hurt." She pauses, considering her words. "A good zoo is how humans **make amends**."

conveniently: We are **conveniently** located off I-95, with shows …

Paragraph Write-up Exercise

Instructions

Write a short paragraph expressing your thoughts about the following questions. There are multiple questions to guide you arrange your thoughts and form your answer. Be sure to answer all the questions within a single paragraph—do not answer the questions individually.

A "paragraph" is a collection of sentences (which are not divided into separate lines) that convey a single idea throughout. The sentences in a paragraph must be logically arranged to coherently deliver your thoughts to the reader. A single paragraph must contain at least three sentences.

Question

What do you think about zoos? Do you think animals are treated well at zoos? Do you think all animals should be freed from zoos? Do you think animals that have lived in a zoo for a long time can survive in the wild if they are released?

Bibliography

1 – "THE REAL IVAN" from *The One and Only Ivan by Katherine Applegate* (https://theoneandonlyivan.com/the-real-ivan)

2 – "Sources of stress in captivity" by K.N. Morgan & C.T. Tromborg in *Applied Animal Behaviour Science* (https://www.sciencedirect.com/science/article/abs/pii/S0168159106001997)

About the Author

Katherine Alice Applegate (65; born Oct 9, 1956) is an American author born in Michigan, U.S. Her specialties are science fiction, fantasy, and adventure novels for children and young adults. Her most well-known works include *The One and Only Ivan*, and the *Animorphs*, *Remnants*, and *Everworld* series.

https://katherineapplegate.com/

Other Books by the Author

Columns of each table: (from left) Title of Book; Year Published; ATOS Book Level; Lexile Measure; Interest Level.

Guide to Interest Level:

LG (Lower Grades; suitable for grades K-3)

MG (Middle Grades; suitable for grades 4-8)

MG+ (Middle Grades Plus; suitable for grades 6+)

UG (Upper Grades; suitable for grades 9-12)

Ivan & Friends Series				
The One and Only Ivan *2013 Newbery Medal	2012	3.6	570L	MG
The One and Only Bob	2020	3.9	570L	MG

Animorphs Seires				
The series consists of 54 books and includes ten companion books.				
Animorphs (54 books)	1996-2001	3.3-4.8	430L-720L	MG
Animorphs Megamorphs (4 books)	1997-2000	3.6-4.0	430L-550L	MG
Animorphs Chronicles (4 books)	1997-2000	4.3-5.1	530L-630L	MG
Animorphs Alternamorphs (2 books)	1999-2000	estimated 5.2 ↓	430L-470L	MG

The Endling Trilogy				
The Last	2018	5.0	690L	MG
The First	2019	5.2	720L	MG
The Only	2021	5.0		MG

Novels				
Home of the Brave	2007	3.5	NP	MG
Crenshaw	2015	3.8	540L	MG
Wishtree	2017	4.2	590L	MG
Willodeen	2021	4.2	610L	MG
Odder	2022			

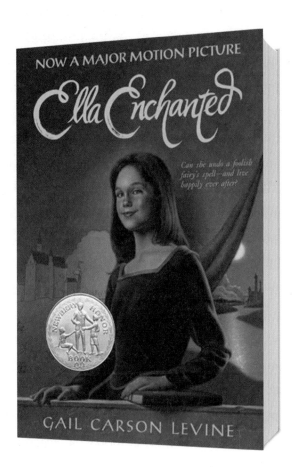

Ella Enchanted

by Gail Carson Levine

Published	1997 (1998 Newbery Honor)
ATOS Book Level	4.6
Lexile	670L
Word Count	52994

Plot Introduction

Have you ever wished for a young-adult version of *Cinderella*? A version where Cinderella attends school and experiences teenage angst? If so, *Ella Enchanted* is just the book for you! Our heroine, Ella, is bewitched with a gift (ahem, *curse*) of obedience at birth. Laid upon her by the unintentionally devious fairy, Lucinda, this "gift" forces Ella to obey all the orders she receives—everything from cleaning her room to surrendering her precious items. After her mother (virtually Ella's *only* caretaker) passes away, Ella enrolls in a boarding school. Unfortunately, all the kids—especially her stepsisters, Hattie and Olive—abuse her curse and make her perform distasteful acts. Frustrated by this, Ella confronts Lucinda at the giants' wedding and asks her to break her curse. However, she refuses to fulfill this request, stating Ella should be *grateful* for her *gift*. Among the adversities, Ella thankfully finds some comfort in Prince Char. After their first encounter at Ella's mother's funeral, they grow closer until romance blossoms between the two. However, when Char asks her to marry him, Ella is compelled to reject, as she is concerned for him and his (soon-to-be) kingdom, owing to her curse. Their relationship takes a turn for the awkward after this rejection, but she continues to think of him every day. Then, one day, Prince Char opens a series of balls to choose his future wife. Still deeply in love with Char, Ella decides to attend these balls *in disguise*, not wanting Char to notice her. However, her identity gets revealed at the final ball, and she runs away to her home. Prince Char follows her and asks her to marry him once again. Will Ella be able to break her curse and accept Char's proposal?

Themes

You know, this book doesn't really have a notable theme that runs through the core of its plot. One idea crystallizes out of the ending: *you can do whatever you put your mind to.* Ella managed to break her curse by resisting an order from Prince Char—when he asked her to marry him, her genuine concern for Char's safety instilled her with enough courage and determination to reject the order. Leading up to this point, whenever Ella attempted to turn down an order, aggressive force swiveled around her, making her dizzy and restless. However, her strong will ultimately allowed her to overcome these adversities and reject Char's order, freeing her from the curse and granting her a happy ending.

Perhaps a bit obscure indirect theme of the book concerns *the power of words*. In the book, many characters hurt Ella with their words (in the form of *orders*). Almost every order that comes Ella's way is irritating and/or even damaging to her. To list a few, Hattie and Olive ordered Ella to surrender her locket necklace (that contains her mother's photo), hand over her lunch money, and even break up with her only friend at school, Arieda. While the book handles this idea solely through Ella obeying orders, we can expand this to how words, *in general*, can hurt people. Especially these days, people nonchalantly leave hurtful comments to strangers on the internet, hiding behind the wall of anonymity. However, we should realize how impactful our words can be—for better or worse—and we must always remember to choose our words carefully.

Questions

1 Summary and First Impressions

   A. Can you give a short summary of the story?

   B. What do you think about the story? Do you like it?

   C. Did you notice that the story is similar to *Cinderella*? Can you point out the similarities between the two stories?

2 Story Questions

   A. What "gift" does Ella receive from Lucinda at birth? How does the spell work?

   B. Who does Ella meet at her mother's funeral and becomes friends with?

   C. How do Hattie and Olive treat Ella at finishing school after discovering that Ella has a curse of obedience? What orders do they give to Ella?

   D. Where does Ella head to when she runs away from finishing school? How does she know that she might find Lucinda there?

   E. When Ella meets Lucinda, what does she ask the fairy to do? What was Lucinda's answer, and how does Ella change after this meeting?

   F. What "gift" does Lucinda give to Sir Peter and Dame Olga at their wedding? How does Dame Olga treat Ella after this, and why?

   G. Why does Ella lie to Prince Char that she plans to marry someone else even though she loves him?

   H. Which events does Ella attend with the help of Mandy and Lucinda? How do they help Ella?

   I. Why does Ella hide her identity at the balls? What does Ella do to keep her identity hidden?

   J. How did Ella's identity get revealed at the balls? What does she do when her identity is revealed?

   K. How does Ella initially answer to Char's proposal? How did that answer break her curse? What happens next, and how does the story end?

③ Character Questions

A. Does Ella have a good sense of humor? Think of how she reacted to Mandy's orders.

B. Does Ella accept her fate and solemnly follow orders, or does she try to rebel? What happens whenever she tries to rebel?

C. Does Ella manage her anger well? How does she express her anger? Is she sarcastic?

D. Is Ella intelligent? Is she good with languages?

E. Is Ella strong and independent?

④ Theme Questions

A. In the story, Ella suffers from the curse of obedience. She has to obey all orders told to her by others.
    Do you have a curse of obedience? Whose words do you obey? Have you ever tried to resist? What happens if you resist?

B. In the form of orders, Ella is regularly hurt by other characters' words. Many of the orders she receives make her perform unfavorable or even dangerous acts. Let's expand this and think about people's "words" in general.
    Do you think words are powerful enough to change or hurt people? Have you had any experiences of getting affected by words deeply?

Vocabulary Exercise

Instructions

These are some words and phrases used in *Ella Enchanted*. Write each of their definition in English. Then, for each word, create your own sentence including that word. Be mindful that one word can have multiple meanings or be used in more than one way. Carefully consider how the words and phrases were used in the original book, and try to use each word/phrase the same way as how the book used it.

Words & Phrases

prevent	observe	resent	delicate	an assortment of
ridicule	describe	admire	especially	persuasive

Sentences from the book

Here are the sentences from the original book that contains the given words and phrases. Only use these as reference and do not write the same sentences for your exercise.

prevent: He could **prevent** anyone from speaking to me or writing to me.

observe: … and stood with the others who **observed** the dance.

resent: I glared at him, **resenting** the order. … It was a game I played with Mandy, obedience and defiance.

delicate: "Hold it **delicately**. It's not a spear. One brings the thread to it."

an assortment of: Sewing Mistress approached, bearing a needle, **an assortment of** colored threads, …

ridicule: "And Sewing Mistress will **ridicule** you if you sew a green rose. Roses have to be red or pink, or yellow if you're daring."

describe: Char continued to **describe** the visit of a trade delegation …

admire: … although most would unmask quickly so he could **admire** their beauty.

especially: Whenever I had time, I practiced the languages, **especially** Ogrese.

persuasive: It sounded **persuasive** to me. I was convinced.

Paragraph Write-up Exercise

Instructions

Write a short paragraph expressing your thoughts about the following questions. There are multiple questions to guide you arrange your thoughts and form your answer. Be sure to answer all the questions within a single paragraph—do not answer the questions individually.

A "paragraph" is a collection of sentences (which are not divided into separate lines) that convey a single idea throughout. The sentences in a paragraph must be logically arranged to coherently deliver your thoughts to the reader. A single paragraph must contain at least three sentences.

Question

Do you think words are powerful enough to hurt other people? Do you think people who hurt others with their words should be punished as seriously as people who hurt others physically? Do you think words also have powerful positive influences as well?

Bibliography

1 – "Interview: World Premiere ELLA ENCHANTED Author Gail Carson Levine Illuminates Magical Worlds" from *Broadway World: Broadway News* (https://www.broadwayworld.com/milwaukee/article/BWW-Interview-World-Premiere-ELLA-ENCHANTED-Author-Gail-Carson-Levine-Illuminates-Magical-Worlds-20160426)

About the Author

Gail Carson Levine (74; born Sep 17, 1947) is an American author born in New York, U.S. Her specialty is fairy tale-fantasy novels for children and young adults. Her most well-known works include *Ella Enchanted*, *The Two Princesses of Bamarre*, and *Fairest*.

https://gailcarsonlevine.com/

Other Books by the Author

Columns of each table: (from left) Title of Book; Year Published; ATOS Book Level; Lexile Measure; Interest Level.

Guide to Interest Level:
LG (Lower Grades; suitable for grades K-3)
MG (Middle Grades; suitable for grades 4-8)
MG+ (Middle Grades Plus; suitable for grades 6+)
UG (Upper Grades; suitable for grades 9-12)

Enchanted Collection				
Ella Enchanted *1998 Newbery Honor	1997	4.6	670L	MG
The Two Princesses of Bamarre	2000	4.5	570L	MG
Fairest	2006	4.1	590L	MG+

Princess Tales				
The Fairy's Mistake	1999	4.0	580L	MG
The Princess Test	1999	4.0	550L	MG
Princess Sonora and the Long Sleep	1999	4.1	650L	MG
Cinderellis and the Glass Hill	2000	4.3	680L	MG
For Biddle's Sake	2002	4.4	770L	MG
The Fairy's Return	2002	3.8	620L	MG

Tale of Two Castles				
A Tale of Two Castles	2011	4.3	630L	MG
Stolen Magic	2015	4.9	670L	MG

Fairies Series				
Fairy Dust and the Quest for the Egg	2005	4.2	660L	LG
Fairy Haven and the Quest for the Wand	2007	3.9	630L	LG
Fairies and the Quest for Never Land	2010	4.0	620L	LG

Novels				
Dave at Night	1999	3.6	550L	MG
The Wish	2000	3.5	490L	MG
Ever	2008	3.7	550L	MG
The Lost Kingdom of Bamarre	2017	4.6	670L	MG
Ogre Enchanted	2018	4.6	630L	MG
A Ceiling Made of Eggshells	2020	4.8	670L	MG
Sparrows in the Wind	2022			

Nonfiction				
Writing Magic: Creating Stories that Fly	2006	5.4	780L	MG
Writer to Writer: From Think to Ink	2014	6.5		MG

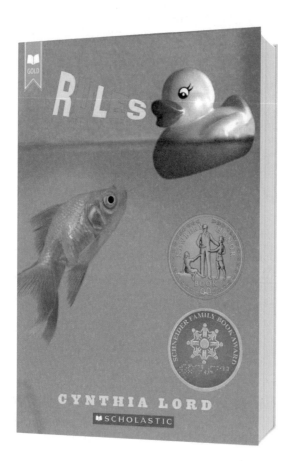

Rules

by Cynthia Lord

Published	2006 (2007 Newbery Honor)
ATOS Book Level	3.9
Lexile	670L
Word Count	31368

Plot Introduction

Closing your eyes isn't going to change anything. Nothing's going to disappear just because you can't see what's going on. – Haruki Murakami, Kafka on the Shore

Well, well, well, here's another book with a heavy topic: *disability*. Disability is undoubtedly tricky to deal with, but we cannot shut our eyes on it either. Even mundane, everyday tasks can be considerably challenging for the disabled, and they deserve everyone's respect. Nevertheless, if *you* had a *disabled sibling* yourself, you might beg to differ—their uncontrollable behaviors and frustrating tantrums may irritate you and hinder your understanding mindset. Meet Catherine, a twelve-year-old girl who just wants a *normal* life. Unfortunately, her life is far from the ordinary because she has an autistic eight-year-old brother, David. As the older sister, it's her responsibility to look after David, no matter how embarrassing and obnoxious it can be. David's symptoms are painfully conspicuous—he regularly screams, gets easily aggravated, and acts shamefully in public. Catherine desperately wishes that David's autism would magically disappear one day. There's some good news for her, though: a girl precisely her age, Kristi, moves in next door. Catherine hopes to become great friends with Kristi and finally get an excuse to be away from David. However, she begins to feel unsure about this friendship after witnessing how Kristi treats David. Catherine also befriends Jason, a boy her age with a neck-down paralyzed body who attends the same therapy clinic as David. While she quickly becomes great friends with Jason, she avoids being seen with him in public, as she feels skeptical about how others—especially Kristi—would perceive her. Who will Catherine realize as her true friend, and how will her thoughts about disabled people change by the end of the book?

Themes

This book provides us with a wonderful opportunity to consider *disability*. It's not rocket science to figure out that disabled people live far more demanding lives than others. And it's not astrophysics to realize that you must not be prejudiced against the disabled and help them as much as possible. But these are *much easier said than done*. Imagine someone who constantly screams and goes on temper tantrums every minute—it'd be arduous to treat him/her like a non-disabled person. However, we should always remember that fundamentally the disabled require more assistance and that their symptoms should never become a source of discrimination or ridicule. After all, none of these people *wished* to be disabled. They deserve massive respect for simply keeping on with their lives—even the simplest daily tasks can be hundreds of times more challenging for our special friends.

Here's an interesting info on the book: according to the author, Cynthia Lord, *Rules* was inspired by her *own* experience. She has two children herself—an older daughter who is non-disabled (like Catherine) and a younger son who has autism (like David). She states that through *Rules*, she wanted to explore her own emotions of having a special son and the dynamics involved within it. She also noted that none of the existing literature about disabled children seems to discuss the beautiful *community* involved. Lord shares that as soon as her son was diagnosed, she was introduced to a brilliant community of special-needs families and professionals with whom she ended up "forming a tight circle." According to her, a so-called "waiting room club" was formed, in which the families shared their children's achievements and congratulated each other while waiting for their therapy sessions. Lord says that, through *Rules*, she wanted to celebrate the difference her family has and highlight all the beautiful things that can occur in one's life for having a child with special needs.

If you dig deeper, you can also find a cue on *friendship*. A healthy friendship is *balanced* and *mutual*; one should not expect or assume any favors from the other. Admittedly, Catherine's thoughts and emotions were heavily influenced by her current situation—with having to constantly take care of David (and not having a single friend around her), it was natural for her to desire love from Kristi. Yet it was inappropriate of her to *assume* that Kristi would provide for her. Having earnest expectations for a relationship usually leads to a bad ending. Instead, focusing on yourself while continuously wishing for each other's best will result in a concrete, synergistic relationship.

In a way, Catherine may have tried *too hard* to become Kristi's friend. In several instances of the plot, we see Catherine admire Kristi's style and appearance. This may simply be Catherine's enthusiastic welcome toward the first-ever friend in her neighborhood, but it appears to be a bit more than that. Catherine seems to *idolize* Kristi—to build her up like she's somehow *superior*. Some may enjoy such reverence at first, but it's bound to make them uneasy. As said, friendship is a dish best served *balanced*—while it's true that you must (at least try to) return as much favor as you receive in a friendship, it's equally valid that there's no reason to give overwhelming love and support to those who neglect it. The world contains all sorts of people—you *cannot*, and therefore *should not*, aim to satisfy everyone.

Questions

① Summary and First Impressions

A. Can you give a short summary of the story?

B. What do you think about the story? Do you like it?

C. Have you ever met or seen anybody with physical or mental disabilities? How do you feel about the disabled?

② Story Questions

A. What disability is David suffering from? How are his acts and thoughts different from other kids his age?

B. What does Catherine think about her brother David? How does she think other people think about David? Why does she keep making rules for him?

C. What disability is Jason suffering from (the book doesn't provide the precise title of his disability; just list the symptoms)? How does he communicate?

D. How does Catherine feel about Kristi moving in next door? Why does she feel that way?

E. What does David do when he (and Catherine) first met Kristi? What does Kristi think about David?

F. What does Catherine think about Kristi's appearance and style? Relatedly, what is Catherine's thoughts on this friendship?

G. How does Ryan treat David? What does he do with his packet of gums when David returns from OT?

H. What does Catherine give to Jason every time she meets him at the clinic? Which activities do they enjoy together (throughout the entire story)?

I. Where does Kristi ask Catherine to come with her (and Ryan)? Why is Catherine unsure when Kristi tells her to bring Jason along?

J. When Jason asks Catherine to take him to the community center dance at his birthday party, what does she say? Why did Jason get angry at her?

K. What does Catherine confess to Jason at the community center dance (about her thoughts on disability, how she thinks other people see David, why she avoided being seen with him in public, etc.)?

L. How does Kristi react to finding out that Jason is disabled? Who does Catherine realize as her true friend after this encounter?

③ Character Questions

A. How does Catherine feel about her brother David? Why does she feel that way?

B. How do Kristi and Ryan treat Jason? How does Catherine treat Jason? Which do you think is the proper way to treat a disabled person?

C. How does Catherine feel about Kristi becoming her neighbor at the start of the book? How does her thoughts change after realizing how Kristi treats disabled people?

D. Why was Catherine afraid to be seen with Jason in public? How did her thoughts change?

④ Theme Questions

A. Catherine made rules to keep David in check. This is because when she *directly* told him not to do something, David would never listen. Instead, when she scolded him using rules, David comfortably complied, treating his life as one elaborate "game" containing the said "rules." David was happy to obey the rules and play this exciting game.

How much do you think about Catherine making rules to control David's behaviors, do you think it's a good idea? Do you think this could work in real life (for actual autistic people)?

B. This book focuses on disability and features multiple characters bearing varied conditions.

Have you ever seen a disabled person in real life? Have you treated them equally to non-disabled people? Do you think disabled people need to be respected?

C. Catherine endures several frustrations throughout the story due to having an autistic sibling. She has to surrender most of her free time to take care of her little brother and face the embarrassment of David's antics out in public.

What do you think it would be like to live with an autistic sibling? How would it be different to having a non-disabled sibling?

Vocabulary Exercise

Instructions

These are some words and phrases used in *Rules*. Write each of their definition in English. Then, for each word, create your own sentence including that word. Be mindful that one word can have multiple meanings or be used in more than one way. Carefully consider how the words and phrases were used in the original book, and try to use each word/phrase the same way as how the book used it.

Words & Phrases

consider	overlap	appointment	suppose	insist
comfort	discuss	communication	announce	mimic

Sentences from the book

Here are the sentences from the original book that contains the given words and phrases. Only use these as reference and do not write the same sentences for your exercise.

consider: Hunting out the window for something to draw, I **consider** the line of stores and restaurants across the street.

overlap: I solved my hating snakes by drawing their scales, tiny and silvery, **overlapping** and **overlapping** …

appointment: … Mom and I walk to the waterfront park while David has his **appointment**.

suppose: 'I'm in this wheelchair, you idiot! How do you *suppose* I am?'

insist: "Jason **insisted** I come back," Mrs. Morehouse says, "and tell you he likes the picture you're drawing."

comfort: "He can't help being afraid!" she snaps. "Why don't *you* **comfort** him? …"

discuss: … and Jason's mother and Mrs. Frost **discuss** good restaurants accommodate wheelchairs.

communication: There's a tray on Jason's wheelchair, and on the tray is a **communication** book.

announce: *If you want to get away with something, don't **announce** it first.*

mimic: *… David laughed and laughed in that twisted position, and Ryan **mimicked** David, tipping his own head way over, laughing.*

Paragraph Write-up Exercise

Instructions

Write a short paragraph expressing your thoughts about the following questions. There are multiple questions to guide you arrange your thoughts and form your answer. Be sure to answer all the questions within a single paragraph—do not answer the questions individually.

A "paragraph" is a collection of sentences (which are not divided into separate lines) that convey a single idea throughout. The sentences in a paragraph must be logically arranged to coherently deliver your thoughts to the reader. A single paragraph must contain at least three sentences.

Question

Search and write the life story of a famous disabled person. The person may be not alive anymore or still alive to this day. Describe how they were treated before they achieved fame, what efforts they put in to overcome their disabilities, and which accomplishments they made in their area. See also if they have provided any help for other disabled people. Express your thoughts on their life.

Bibliography

1 – "Author Interview: Cynthia Lord on Rules" from *Cynthia Leitich Smith*
(https://cynthialeitichsmith.com/2006/03/author-interview-cynthia-lord-on-rules/)

About the Author

Cynthia Lord (72; born in 1950) is an American author born in Massachusetts, U.S. Her specialty is heartwarming, slice-of-life novels for children and young adults. Her most well-known works include *Rules* and *Hot Rod Hamster*.

https://www.cynthialord.com/

Other Books by the Author

Columns of each table: (from left) Title of Book; Year Published; ATOS Book Level; Lexile Measure; Interest Level.

Guide to Interest Level:

LG (Lower Grades; suitable for grades K-3)

MG (Middle Grades; suitable for grades 4-8)

MG+ (Middle Grades Plus; suitable for grades 6+)

UG (Upper Grades; suitable for grades 9-12)

Novels				
Rules *2007 Newbery Honor	2006	3.9	670L	MG
Touch Blue	2010	4.4	750L	MG
Half a Chance	2014	4.5	690L	MG
A Handful of Stars	2015	4.4	690L	MG
Because of the Rabbit	2019	4.3	660L	MG

A Wrinkle in Time

by Madeleine L'Engle

Published	1962 (1963 Newbery Medal)
ATOS Book Level	4.7
Lexile	740L
Word Count	49965

Plot Introduction

Have you ever wanted to explore the universe? Have you ever wanted to visit other planets? Well, this beautiful story brings that thrilling experience to you. The plot is led by three protagonists: Meg, her little brother Charles, and her friend Calvin. Meg's father is trapped on a planet called Camazotz—lightyears away from earth, under control by the "Dark Thing." Reminiscent of a shadow, the Dark Thing is pure evil and puts innocent stars and planets in danger by brainwashing their inhabitants. Upon learning this, Meg decides she must rescue her father and embarks on a journey with Charles and Calvin. Her party is accompanied by the three Mrs. W's: Mrs. Whatsit, Mrs. Who, and Mrs. Which—they are ex-star witches that live in the forest and can travel through the universe using a bizarre technique called "tessering." Once the children arrive at Camazotz, they're directed to a tall building called the "CENTRAL Central Intelligence." There, they encounter a strange man with red eyes who hypnotizes Charles in exchange for disclosing the location of Meg's father. Despite the resistance of 'possessed Charles,' Meg successfully liberates her father from his prison cell. Possessed Charles then leads the party to IT, the physical incarnation of the Dark Thing that takes the form of a giant disembodied brain. The party learns that IT controls Camazotz's citizens by radiating a powerful, rhythmical pulse that forces everybody to act in perfect sync. Just before IT seizes control of Meg's mind, Meg's father tessers out of Camazotz, taking Meg and Calvin with him. Unfortunately, Charles must be left behind as he is still in IT's grip. Will Meg be able to save Charles from IT and return safely back to earth?

Themes

Just like *Ella Enchanted* a couple of chapters ago, *A Wrinkle in Time* doesn't have a discernable "theme." Instead, we can extract some meaningful ideas from segments of the book. The first comes from when the children first arrive at Camazotz. There, they each received a few gifts to aid their journey on the hazardous planet. Meg received something peculiar that annoyed her: *her faults*. She had an assortment of them, such as short temper, impatience, and stubbornness, none of which she had ever considered helpful. On the grand scheme of things, however, Meg's faults ironically ended up assisting her throughout her journey—her short temper and sharp anger allowed her to repel IT's grip, and her impatience and stubbornness granted her to stay focused on her mission, avoiding all the alluring distractions on Camazotz. As ridiculous as it may sound, your fault may act as an advantage depending on the situation (and perspective). What about you? What do you think are your faults? Can you think of a case where your faults can help you?

Now let's consider the three main characters of the book—Meg, Charles, and Calvin. If you think about it, each of them is who we would generally consider a "misfit." Meg struggles to find confidence in her looks and personality, so she prefers to be alone. She's also outcasted at school by her unorthodox ways of solving math problems. Next, Charles is a genius—he knows way more than any other child his age and can even read others' minds if he tries. But he knows it's better to "act dumb" and stay under the radar, so he opts to play the silent game. Finally, Calvin has gifted athleticism and is talented at many activities (unlike his ten siblings). Hence, he constantly feels he doesn't belong in the family. As you can see, sometimes the misfits are *not* the weird ones—they could, in fact, be highly talented individuals. After all, uniqueness is where mind-blowing changes stem from; if everyone looked and acted the same, our world would be nothing more than the depressingly dull Camazotz.

As a minor addendum, a distinct rain of Christianity reportedly wets the book. Principally, the running theme of good vs. evil (light vs. darkness) represents this aspect. For example, the book displays a star emitting extremely bright light to overcome the Dark Thing at one point. Furthermore, the ultimate weapon Meg used to defeat IT was *love*—something continuously emphasized in Christianity.

Questions

1 Summary and First Impressions

A. Can you give a short summary of the story?

B. What do you think about the story? Do you like it?

C. Do you believe that "tessering" (a combination of time-travel and teleportation) right can become reality one day? If you could "tesser" now, how would you use the technique?

2 Story Questions

A. At the start of the story, where was Meg's father, Mr. Murry, at? How did he get there? What did the townspeople think had happened to him?

B. When Meg and Charles first met Calvin, why did he tell them he was there? Can you describe how his mother is like (especially to her children)?

C. How does Meg describe the feeling of tessering, after she experiences it for the first time?

D. Where (i.e., which planet) do the Mrs. W's take the children to first by tessering? What does Mrs. Whatsit show the children there?

E. To whom do the Mrs. W's take the children to next? What does the person show the children through the crystal ball?

F. After looking at Happy Medium's crystal ball, what do the children learn about the Mrs. W's (and their identities)?

G. Where do the Mrs. W's take the children to next? Why did they take the children there?

H. How is tessering to Camazotz different from the previous instances for Meg? Why does it feel different for her?

I. What gifts do the Mrs. W's give to the children on Camazotz? Describe what each received, one by one. What advice do they give to the children?

J. What stands out about the houses and the buildings of Camazotz? What stands out about the inhabitants of Camazotz and how they act?

K. Who do the children meet at the CENTRAL Central Intelligence? What does the person do to Charles?

L. Where was Mr. Murry captured in, and how did Meg get to him?

M. How did Calvin use his gift (from the Mrs. W's) to distract possessed Charles, allowing Meg to get to her father?

N. What was IT's identity? How did IT affect Meg as she got closer to it? How did Meg, Calvin, and Mr. Murry escape from IT (leaving Charles on Camazotz for the moment)?

O. Who do Meg, Calvin, and Mr. Murry meet on Ixchel? How do they help the three?

P. Why is Meg the only one who can save Charles? How did she overcome IT's power and save Charles?

Q. What happens after Meg saves Charles, and how does the story end?

③ **Character Questions**

A. How would you describe Meg's personalities? Is she loving and caring? Is she smart?

B. What are Meg's faults? How does she use these to her advantage while she journeys through Camazotz?

C. How is Charles Wallace different from other five-year-old kids? What are his faults?

D. Describe Calvin. What does his family think about him? Does he also have any special talents like Charles or Meg?

E. Who are Mrs. Whatsit, Mrs. Which, and Mrs. Who? Where do they live? What did they used to be a long time ago?

F. What is IT? How does IT control the people of Camazotz?

A. The scenery in Camazotz is so peculiar that it's almost disturbing—everyone behaves the same and carries the same thoughts. Admittedly, this is due to IT's influence over the planet. But, let's think about this uniformity in general terms.

Do you think everybody will be happy if they all behaved the same and had the same thought as each other? Do you think you can still be happy even if you're different from everyone else?

B. To aid her adventure through Camazotz, the three children each receive some gifts. Meg, of other things, receives her faults as gifts. While she is initially disappointed by this, they end up helping her on the dangerous planet—her short temper allowed her to resist IT's grips, while her stubbornness allowed her to focus on her mission.

Do you think your faults (i.e., traits you don't like about yourself) could be helpful in some situations? Describe a fault of yours and give a case where it can come in handy.

Vocabulary Exercise

Instructions

These are some words and phrases used in *A Wrinkle in Time*. Write each of their definition in English. Then, for each word, create your own sentence including that word. Be mindful that one word can have multiple meanings or be used in more than one way. Carefully consider how the words and phrases were used in the original book, and try to use each word/phrase the same way as how the book used it.

Words & Phrases

vicious	give in	supposed to	delighted	appropriate (*adj.*)
eager	nervously	permission	stubborn	take [*n.*] for granted

Sentences from the book

Here are the sentences from the original book that contains the given words and phrases. Only use these as reference and do not write the same sentences for your exercise.

vicious: Surely her mother must know what people were saying, must be aware of the smugly **vicious** gossip.

give in: "… You see, on this planet, everything is in perfect order because everybody has learned to relax, to **give in**, to submit …"

supposed to & permission: "… you're not **supposed to** go off our property without **permission** …"

delighted: "… I like him very much, and I'm **delighted** he's found his way here."

appropriate (*adj.*): He had orange hair that needed cutting and the **appropriate** freckles to go with it.

eager: … **eager** to get into the town. "Let's hurry," she begged, "*please!* Don't you want to find Father?"

nervously: Meg looked **nervously** to where Mrs. Whatsit had been standing … But Mrs. Whatsit was no longer there.

stubborn: So when they want her to do problems the long way around at school, she gets sullen and **stubborn** …

take [*n*.] for granted: "I guess I never thought of that. I guess I just **took it for granted**."

Paragraph Write-up Exercise

Instructions

Write a short paragraph expressing your thoughts about the following questions. There are multiple questions to guide you arrange your thoughts and form your answer. Be sure to answer all the questions within a single paragraph—do not answer the questions individually.

A "paragraph" is a collection of sentences (which are not divided into separate lines) that convey a single idea throughout. The sentences in a paragraph must be logically arranged to coherently deliver your thoughts to the reader. A single paragraph must contain at least three sentences.

Question

What do you think are your faults? Can you think of a situation where one (or more) of your faults can come in handy? Explain why.

Bibliography

About the Author

Madeleine L'Engle (born Nov 29, 1918; died Sep 6 2007, aged 88) was an American writer born in New York, U.S. Her specialties were fictions, non-fictions, and poetries based on modern science with hints of Christianity. She is most well-known for her *A Wrinkle in Time* series: *A Wrinkle in Time, A Wind in the Door, A Swiftly Tilting Planet, Many Waters*, and *An Acceptable Time*.

https://www.madeleinelengle.com/

Other Books by the Author

Columns of each table: (from left) Title of Book; Year Published; ATOS Book Level; Lexile Measure; Interest Level.

Guide to Interest Level:
LG (Lower Grades; suitable for grades K-3)
MG (Middle Grades; suitable for grades 4-8)
MG+ (Middle Grades Plus; suitable for grades 6+)
UG (Upper Grades; suitable for grades 9-12)

Time Quintet				
A Wrinkle in Time *1963 Newbery Medal	1962	4.7	740L	MG
A Wind in the Door	1973	5.0	790L	MG
A Swiftly Tilting Planet	1978	5.2	850L	MG
Many Waters	1986	4.7	700L	MG
An Acceptable Time	1989	4.5	710L	MG+

Austin Family Chronicles Series				
Meet the Austins	1960	5.3	1010L	UG
The Moon by Night	1963	5.5	940L	UG
The Young Unicorns	1968	6.5	820L	UG
A Ring of Endless Light *1981 Newbery Honor	1980	5.2	810L	UG
Troubling a Star	1994	5.1	850L	UG

O'Keefe Family Series				
The Arm of the Starfish	1965	5.5	860L	MG+
Dragons in the Waters	1976	5.5	830L	MG+
A House Like a Lotus	1984	5.0	790L	MG+

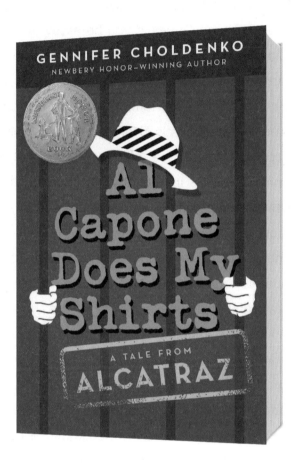

Al Capone Does My Shirts

by Gennifer Choldenko

Published	2004 (2005 Newbery Honor)
ATOS Book Level	3.5
Lexile	600L
Word Count	49509

Plot Introduction

How would you feel if you lived next to an active prison? Would you be excited in the vicinity of high-profile criminals? Or would you be afraid that they might escape and harm you? Either way, you'd probably consider living next to a jailhouse a notable perk. But, our protagonist, Moose Flannagan, has something more pressing to worry about: his autistic older sister, Natalie. The year is 1935; Moose's family moves to Alcatraz Island—a small island in San Francisco Bay that houses the notorious Alcatraz Prison. Two kilometers off the nearest shore, it's practically impossible to escape Alcatraz, making it the perfect place to accommodate the worst convicts across the country. The main motive of the move was to secure Natalie a seat in Esther P. Marinoff—a special-needs school on the island known for its excellent cure rates. Moose isn't pleased about the move because he has to transfer, but he thankfully adapts to his new school quickly. Unfortunately, Natalie doesn't adjust to *her* new school smoothly and is dispelled from Esther P. Marinoff only days after her admission. Now, Moose has to look after Natalie and take her everywhere he goes. While this seriously annoys Moose, it helps Natalie enormously—meeting Moose's friends and experiencing a "normal" life improves her condition immaculately (especially her *speech*). Delighted by this change, Moose's mother is convinced that if Natalie reapplies for Esther P. Marinoff, she will secure a seat once and for all. Unfortunately, Natalie gets rejected once more, for the school realizes she is too old for their programs. Frustrated by this, Moose decides to ask for help from one of Alcatraz's most influential prisoners, Al Capone. Will Moose acquire the help he needs?

Themes

Al Capone Does My Shirts has a peculiar structure: while the book primarily walks along a central storyline—Natalie's struggles with her autism—it contains several episodic events—such as the Alcatraz laundry service, the convict baseball, and Al Capone's mother's visit. Interestingly, none of these side stories closely relate to the book's main plot. Perhaps the book's loose diary-style narrative contributes to this architecture as well. As a result, there aren't too many themes to consider regarding the entire book.

The book presents another opportunity for us to think about *the disabled*. Just like in *Rules*, we have a character struggling with autism, Natalie. However, the discussion offered in *Al Capone Does My Shirts* is slightly different from those from *Rules*. While *Rules* guided us to consider how non-disabled people should treat disabled people, *Al Capone Does My Shirts* suggests we contemplate *what kind of life would benefit the disabled the most*. Albeit for Natalie's admission into Esther P. Marinoff, Moose's parents hide several plain facts about their daughter from herself. For example, they try to make her believe that she is a lot younger than she actually is and that she is not disabled. We later learn that Natalie knew the truth all along—she just followed her parents' plans even so. It is understandable to avoid entirely disclosing all the symptoms to the disabled. But it could also be hurtful when they are already *well aware* of their disability and realize that everyone's trying to hide it from them. In truth, most of the time, *they know* (that they're disabled)—however, they are often ashamed of it and have difficulties clearly expressing themselves. Perhaps being blunt about their symptoms could help them accept their disability and inspire them to try to overcome it.

Here's another idea about disability to chew on—*is it better to subject the disabled to therapies, or is it better to let them pursue ordinary lives?* Therapies are deliberately designed for the disabled by certified professionals, but there are also many things they can learn from just living "normal" lives. Indeed, should their disability be too severe, therapies may be the only option. But otherwise, simply observing how non-disabled people speak and behave could improve the disabled's condition significantly.

Okay, this is the *last* point about disability: *are special needs schools effective?* As explained, an ordinary life could benefit the disabled unexpectedly much; however, a "normal life" cannot be achieved if disabled students are grouped up with each other. To mix them in with non-disabled students is essential to provide them with truly "normal" lives. Then again, special needs schools have teachers specifically trained to handle disabled students; the teachers of general schools may struggle with even a single disabled student. Not to mention how disabled students could become the target of bullying by non-disabled students.

An extra bitesize topic in this book is *family and parenting*. Though perfectly understandable—due to Natalie's conditions—Moose is comparatively shunned by his parents. This leads to a sizable three-way argument between Moose, his dad, and his mom at Natalie's birthday party. Naturally, each child in a family should receive the same amount of love and care. But what if one *surely* needs more than the other?

Questions

(1) Summary and First Impressions

A. Can you give a short summary of the story?

B. What do you think about the story? Do you like it?

C. What do you think it would be like to live next to an active prison? How would it be different from living in a normal neighborhood?

(2) Story Questions

A. Why did Moose's family move to Alcatraz? Why does his sister, Natalie, need to go to a special school?

B. What place is the Esther P. Marinoff School? What kind of students attend the school?

C. What are the rules on Alcatraz Island for its inhabitants (as the Warden tells Moose when he first meets him)?

D. What kind of work/chores do the convicts do for the inhabitants of Alcatraz Island?

E. What service does Piper suggest Moose to offer their school kids? Why does she want to offer such a service? Why does she think this service would be popular among the school kids?

F. On Moose's first school day, what news does he hear from the Esther P. Marinoff School about Natalie? What happens to Natalie next?

G. What kind of tests and programs had Natalie gone through? How did they impact the Flanagans?

H. After Natalie gets kicked out of the Esther P. Marinoff School, where is she sent to? What does Moose's mother start doing at this point, and what does Moose have to do for his sister?

I. How do Piper and Moose advertise their Alcatraz Laundry Service? What were the kids' reaction at first, and how did it change after they received their laundered clothes? Why did their reaction change so?

J. How does the Warden find out about the kids' laundry service, and what does he say to them?

K. Why does Moose go looking for the convict baseballs? How does he obtain one, and what does he do with it?

L. Who is Convict 105, a.k.a. "Onion," and why is Moose worried about him and Natalie being close?

M. How does Natalie change after undergoing Mrs. Kelly's therapy, especially in how she talks? What has Moose's mom got to say about this?

N. Why do Moose and his mother have an argument at Natalie's birthday party? Why does Moose demand that his parents reveal Natalie's true age?

O. What response does Natalie get from Esther P. Marinoff after taking the entrance interview for the second time? Why did she receive such an answer?

P. What does Moose decide to do about Natalie failing her entrance interview? How does his plan work out?

③ Character Questions

A. Is Moose sincere and obedient to his parents or malicious and rebellious?

B. What illness does Natalie have? What are her symptoms? What does she like doing and what does she excel at?

C. Does Moose love his sister Natalie? Does he try to give her the best? Is he responsible?

D. Why do Mr. and Mrs. Flanagan work so hard? Do they treat Moose and Natalie differently? How does Moose feel about this?

E. What does Mr. Flanagan realize about the relationship between Moose and his mother (at, and after Natalie's sixteenth birthday party)? Does Mrs. Flanagan treat Moose differently after talking with her husband?

A. Back in *Rules*, we witnessed the struggles of having a *younger* sibling with autism. In *Al Capone Does My Shirts*, we see the struggles of having an *older* sibling with autism.

Which do you think would be more difficult—having a *younger* sibling with autism or an *older* sibling with autism? Why?

B. Just like Esther P. Marinoff in this book, there are many "special-needs schools" that are specifically designed for disabled students in real life. In them, students of varied disabilities and symptoms are grouped up into one class. Usually, these schools employ teachers who have received professional training in treating disabled people, and each class is often led by multiple teachers. While the disabled students can get focused care, they would miss out on the opportunity to play with non-disabled students.

What do you think about special-needs schools that group disabled students into one class? Do you think it's a good idea, or do you think disabled students should mix in with non-disabled students?

C. In the book, Moose's parents hide Natalie's real age from her. A part of this felt like to make her believe she's young enough to enter Esther P. Marinoff. But, a part of this also felt like to make Natalie believe she's still young and has a chance of overcoming her disabilities. For whichever reason it was, it turns out Natalie knew her exact age all along. Just imagine how ridiculous she would have considered having to pretend she's a lot younger than she actually is.

What do you think about hiding facts about them or their condition against a disabled person? Is it not a good idea to be completely honest with a disabled person about their situation?

Vocabulary Exercise

Instructions

These are some words and phrases used in *Al Capone Does My Shirts*. Write each of their definition in English. Then, for each word, create your own sentence including that word. Be mindful that one word can have multiple meanings or be used in more than one way. Carefully consider how the words and phrases were used in the original book, and try to use each word/phrase the same way as how the book used it.

Words & Phrases

convict	reputation	apparently	all of a sudden
build [n.] up	impressive	desperate	be involved with
not a thing in sight		as far as I'm concerned	

Sentences from the book

Here are the sentences from the original book that contains the given words and phrases. Only use these as reference and do not write the same sentences for your exercise.

convict: The **convicts** we have are the kind other prisons don't want.

reputation: "You're getting a bad **reputation** with the girls!"

apparently & desperate: I never thought I'd care about bowling … But **apparently** I'm **desperate**, because whenever Theresa's mom doesn't need her to help with baby Rocky, we take Natalie down to the bowling alley …

all of a sudden: "How come you're so friendly with her **all of a sudden**?"

build [n.] up: We've **built [the Esther P. Marinoff] up** like it's quite the place.

impressive: "This school has skilled teachers working with these kids around the clock. It's an **impressive** place."

be involved with: "Oh, no, Moose would never **be involved with** something like that."

not a thing in sight: "… the Esther P. Marinoff School, where … and there **isn't a chalkboard or a book in sight**."

as far as I'm concerned: "**As far as I'm concerned**, 105 does not exist."

Paragraph Write-up Exercise

Instructions

Write a short paragraph expressing your thoughts about the following questions. There are multiple questions to guide you arrange your thoughts and form your answer. Be sure to answer all the questions within a single paragraph—do not answer the questions individually.

A "paragraph" is a collection of sentences (which are not divided into separate lines) that convey a single idea throughout. The sentences in a paragraph must be logically arranged to coherently deliver your thoughts to the reader. A single paragraph must contain at least three sentences.

Question

Do you think it is a good idea to put all the disabled students in one class? Do you think a disabled person would learn more by living an ordinary life than by going through therapies? If you had a disabled friend in your class at school, how would you help him/her? (If you already have one, how are you helping him/her?)

Bibliography

About the Author

Gennifer Choldenko (64; born Oct 20, 1957) is an American children and young-adults' author born in California, U.S. She is most well-known for her *Al Capone* series: *Al Capone Does My Shirts*, *Al Capone Shines My Shoes*, *Al Capone Does My Homework*, and *Al Capone Throws Me a Curve*.

https://choldenko.com/

Other Books by the Author

Columns of each table: (from left) Title of Book; Year Published; ATOS Book Level; Lexile Measure; Interest Level.

Guide to Interest Level:

LG (Lower Grades; suitable for grades K-3)

MG (Middle Grades; suitable for grades 4-8)

MG+ (Middle Grades Plus; suitable for grades 6+)

UG (Upper Grades; suitable for grades 9-12)

Tales from Alcatraz Series				
Al Capone Does My Shirts *2005 Newbery Honor	2004	3.5	600L	MG
Al Capone Shines My Shoes	2009	3.8	620L	MG
Al Capone Does My Homework	2013	3.7	570L	MG
Al Capone Throws Me a Curve	2018	3.7	540L	MG

Novels				
Notes from a Liar and Her Dog	2001	3.8	580L	MG
If a Tree Falls at Lunch Period	2007	3.0	530L	MG
No Passengers Beyond This Point	2011	3.9	620L	MG
Chasing Secrets	2015	3.7	540L	MG
One-Third Nerd	2019	3.6	540L	MG
Orphan Eleven	2020	4.3	640L	MG

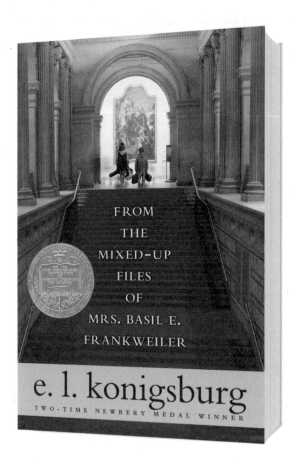

From the Mixed-Up Files of Mrs. Basil E. Frankweiler

by E. L. Konigsburg

Published	1967 (1968 Newbery Medal)
ATOS Book Level	4.7
Lexile	700L
Word Count	30906

Plot Introduction

Have you ever had the urge to run away from home? I bet everyone considers it at least once in their lives—some earlier than others. For Claudia, our heroine today, the thought comes to her at twelve years of age. Claudia is not too pleased about how she is treated at home—she feels unfair that she must bear so many responsibilities as the oldest child and the only daughter in the house. Well, she claims so, but it seems like the real problem is: she needs a *spark*—Claudia is sick and tired of the sameness of every day. To kickstart her engines, Claudia makes her escape with one of her little brothers, Jamie (who was brought along for financial and mental support). While it might sound spontaneous, she actually planned her escape meticulously. She wanted her getaway to be grand and graceful—hence she selected her destination: the Metropolitan Museum of Art. Upon arrival, Claudia becomes absorbed in an exciting mystery: the Met has recently purchased a new marble statue that is speculated to be the work of the Italian Renaissance master Michelangelo himself! Even experts have yet to prove this, and anyone who finds evidence would secure a sizable prize. Claudia and Jamie decide to do some digging—they consult books about Michelangelo at the library and discover what seems to be Michelangelo's signature on the statue. Unfortunately, all their efforts render fruitless. On the verge of giving up, Claudia impulsively decides to visit and question the statue's seller—Mrs. Basil E. Frankweiler—directly. Will Claudia and Jamie find decisive evidence and solve this enticing mystery?

Themes

What makes you feel special? What makes you feel unique? What makes you feel different from the others? For Claudia, it's *secrets*—to know something that others do not. She embarked on this journey to feel different, to *be* different; she wanted to return home as a different person. For that, she needed something that could transform her and set her apart from everyone else. Traversing through the Angel mystery, Claudia realized that obtaining and holding secrets is what makes her unique. That's why she was satisfied with the final deal with Mrs. Frankweiler even though it did not grant her immediate wealth. Since Mrs. Frankweiler decided to bestow the "proof" (i.e., the sketch of Angel signed by Michelangelo) through her will, Claudia would not lay her hands on it until Mrs. Frankweiler passed away. And, of course, the proof is imperative for Claudia to secure her fame and wealth. However, she is pleased with this deal because the money and the fame are not what she's after—she's after the *secret*; the crux of the bargain for Claudia is that she gained a marvelous secret. Many different *objects*, *thoughts*, and *activities* can make us feel one-of-a-kind. It could also be an *ability* you have—being exceptionally skilled at a sport or knowledgeable about a subject at school could make you feel unique. What about you? What makes you unique?

Approaching from a different point of view, this book also offers a discussion on *secrets*. How do secrets make one feel special? Does it still count even if no one else knows about it? If no one knows you're keeping a secret, is it even a "secret" anymore? To take the book's case as an example: had Claudia deciphered the mystery herself without anyone else knowing about it—not even Jamie—would she still have been satisfied? Would she still have been happy? Would she still have felt like she returned home as a different person? In other news, is it okay to keep secrets from people? Some things may be better left untold, especially if it includes sensitive or personal information about individuals. But is it impolite or even immoral to keep secrets against specific people?

One more idea we can briefly consider is: *running away from home*. Just like "the reasons for feeling unique," there could be millions of different motives that drive you to escape your haven. But your home is undoubtedly the most comfortable and secure place you could be. What kind of dissatisfaction or frustration could possibly lead you to move out of such a hospitable environment? Maybe you've already felt the urge to run away from home. Why did you feel that way? And do you think it would be worth it?

Questions

1 Summary and First Impressions

   A. Can you give a short summary of the story?

   B. What do you think about the story? Do you like it?

   C. Do you enjoy visiting museums? What do you think it would be like to live inside a museum for a week? Would you like to try?

2 Story Questions

   A. Why did Claudia decide to run away from her home?

   B. Where did Claudia decide to head after running away from home? Why did she choose the place?

   C. Who did Claudia decide to take with her and why? How does he have so much money?

   D. Describe Claudia and Jamie's trip to the Metropolitan Museum of Art. How did they initially escape home, and how did they get to the museum?

   E. How did Claudia and Jamie avoid the guards during the shifts (twice a day, once when the museum opens and once when the museum closes)? How did they stay undetected during the night time?

   F. Describe Claudia and Jamie's life at the Metropolitan Museum of Art. Where did they sleep? What did they eat? How did they manage their belongings? How did they wash themselves and their clothes? What did they do during the daytime?

   G. What did Claudia and Jamie see when they first visited the Italian Renaissance Hall? Why were there so many people interested in the art piece?

   H. Why did Claudia want to purchase a New York Times newspaper? What did the newspaper article say about the *Angel*? What did the article say about Mrs. Basil E. Frankweiler?

   I. What happened to the *Angel* the next day, after the museum closed? What did

Claudia and Jamie find on the pedestal where the statue used to stand? What did the marking mean?

J. Who did Claudia and Jamie decide to inform about the symbol? What response did they get from the person?

K. After Claudia and Jamie leave the Metropolitan Museum of Art, where do they head to? Why do they go there?

L. When Mrs. Frankweiler asked about the runaway, what did Claudia tell her? Had it made any different to her (yet)? What did Claudia say was the most fun part of running away?

M. When Claudia asks for the details of Angel, what deal does Mrs. Frankweiler offer her? How did Claudia and Jamie find the correct file?

N. What was included in the file they had found? What did the contents mean?

O. What deal did Mrs. Frankweiler make regarding the file? Was she going to give it to the kids right away? If not, how and when were the kids going to receive the file?

P. Why was Claudia pleased even though she did not receive the sketch immediately? What was truly the most important part of running away for her?

③ Character Questions

A. Is Claudia thorough? Does she love making plans?

B. Does Claudia want to stand out? What makes her feel unique, and why?

C. Is Claudia focused and spirited? Does she give up easily?

D. How are Claudia and Mrs. Frankweiler similar? Do they both like to collect secrets and rare information?

④ Theme Questions

A. At the start of the book, Claudia feels the urge to escape from her house because she's not satisfied with her life at home. She feels unfair that she has to do all the chores around the house, being the oldest child and the only girl in the house. Have you ever felt like running away from your home? If you have, why did/do you feel so? Where do you think you would head if you run away?

B. In the book, having secrets makes Claudia feel one-of-a-kind—to know important and/or fascinating facts that no one else knows makes Claudia feel special. Do you like to keep secrets? Do you think secrets become no longer special if nobody knows that you are keeping them? Do you think it's okay to keep secrets related to a particular person against them?

Vocabulary Exercise

Instructions

These are some words and phrases used in *From the Mixed-up Files of Mrs. Basil E. Frankweiler*. Write each of their definition in English. Then, for each word, create your own sentence including that word. Be mindful that one word can have multiple meanings or be used in more than one way. Carefully consider how the words and phrases were used in the original book, and try to use each word/phrase the same way as how the book used it.

Words & Phrases

concentrate	emerge	in front of	intrigue	startled (*adj.*)
postpone	despise	ought to	offer	out of the ordinary

Sentences from the book

Here are the sentences from the original book that contains the given words and phrases. Only use these as reference and do not write the same sentences for your exercise.

concentrate: "… We just won't learn everything about everything. We'll **concentrate** on Michelangelo."

emerge: Jamie would wait twelve minutes (lag time, Claudia called it) and **emerge** from hiding.

in front of: … a piece of Jamie's head plus the coat of the man **in front of** Jamie.

intrigue: He felt certain that mentioning the Italian Renaissance had **intrigued** me.

startled (*adj.*): Both children looked up at me **startled**.

postpone: It would **postpone** her running away only twenty-seven cents worth.

despise: On Saturdays, Claudia emptied the wastebaskets, a task she **despised**.

ought to: "We probably have no conscience. I think we **ought to** be homesick …"

offer: Then Jamie began to feel that the Metropolitan offered **several** advantages …

out of the ordinary: They realized that they were approaching something **out of the ordinary** when they saw a newspaper cameraman walking along the edge of the crowd.

Paragraph Write-up Exercise

Instructions

Write a short paragraph expressing your thoughts about the following questions. There are multiple questions to guide you arrange your thoughts and form your answer. Be sure to answer all the questions within a single paragraph—do not answer the questions individually.

A "paragraph" is a collection of sentences (which are not divided into separate lines) that convey a single idea throughout. The sentences in a paragraph must be logically arranged to coherently deliver your thoughts to the reader. A single paragraph must contain at least three sentences.

Question

What makes you feel different from others? (What makes you feel unique?) How, and why does it make you feel different?

Bibliography

About the Author

Elaine Lobl Konigsburg (born Feb 10, 1930; died Apr 19, 2013, aged 83) was an American author and illustrator born in New York, U.S. Her specialty was coming-of-age, teenage-struggles novels for children and young adults. She illustrated many of her own books. Her most well-known works include *From the Mixed-Up Files of Mrs. Basil E. Frankweiler*, *The View from Saturday*, and *Silent to the Bone*.

Official Publisher Page

https://www.simonandschuster.com/authors/E-L-Konigsburg/20030386

Other Books by the Author

Columns of each table: (from left) Title of Book; Year Published; ATOS Book Level; Lexile Measure; Interest Level.

Guide to Interest Level:
LG (Lower Grades; suitable for grades K-3)
MG (Middle Grades; suitable for grades 4-8)
MG+ (Middle Grades Plus; suitable for grades 6+)
UG (Upper Grades; suitable for grades 9-12)

Novels				
Jennifer, Hecate, Macbeth, William McKinley, and Me, Elizabeth *1968 Newbery Honor	1967	4.5	680L	MG
From the Mixed-up Files of Mrs Basil E. Frankweiler *1968 Newbery Medal	1967	4.7	700L	MG
(George)	1970	5.3		MG
About the B'Nai Bagels	1971	4.7	700L	MG
A Proud Taste for Scarlet and Miniver	1973	5.4	770L	MG
The Dragon in the Ghetto Caper	1974	4.9	730L	MG

The Second Mrs. Giaconda	1975	5.7	840L	MG
Father's Arcane Daughter	1976	5.0	700L	MG
Journey to an 800 Number	1982	4.7	730L	MG
Up from Jericho Tel	1986	5.7	910L	MG
Amy Elizabeth Explores Bloomingdale's	1992	4.4	NC860L	LG
T-backs, T-shirts, Coat, and Suit	1993	5.4	820L	UG
The View from Saturday *1997 Newbery Medal	1996	5.9	870L	NG
Silent to the Bone	2000	5.4	810L	UG
The Outcasts of 19 Schuyler Place	2004	5.5	840L	MG
The Mysterious Edge of the Heroic World	2007	5.7	910L	MG

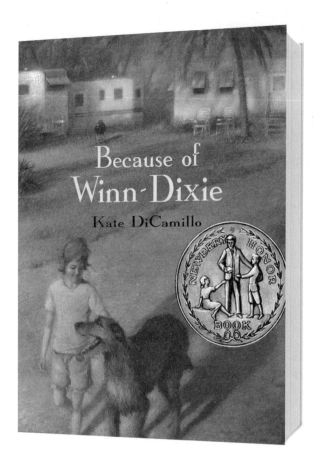

Because of Winn-Dixie

by Kate DiCamillo

Published	2000 (2001 Newbery Honor)
ATOS Book Level	3.9
Lexile	670L
Word Count	22123

Plot Introduction

They say, "a dog is a man's best friend," but there won't be many dogs quite as good at making friends as Winn-Dixie. His goofiness is a weapon that never fails to 'break the ice.' Our heroine today, Opal Buloni, is the owner of Winn-Dixie, and she enjoys the privilege of having such a brilliant conversation starter to the maximum. Opal's been having difficulties making friends after she and her preacher father moved to Naomi, Florida. Opal's relationship with her father is unstable—she disapproves of him, for he could not keep her mother from leaving when Opal was little. One day, Opal visits the local Winn-Dixie grocery store and runs into Winn-Dixie, the lovable pup. Winn-Dixie was causing a scene inside the grocery store—running around and knocking everything off the shelves. Upon hearing the store owner wishes to send the stray away to a pound, Opal impulsively announces that he's her dog and his name is Winn-Dixie. After some persuasion, she manages to earn her father's approval and adopt the dog. From then on, Opal meets many wonderful people in Naomi and befriends them *because of Winn-Dixie*—people just cannot resist his charm! Opal gets particularly familiar with the lovely kindhearted librarian, Miss Franny, the wise and gentle gardener, Gloria Dump, and the timid but sincere pet store cleric, Otis. Near the end of the book, Opal decides to hold a party in Gloria's garden with all her new friends. During the party, a thunderstorm arrives, and Winn-Dixie (who's pathologically afraid of thunderstorms) disappears. As Opal sets out to search for Winn-Dixie with her father, they begin to restore their relationship. Will Opal find Winn-Dixie and straighten out her relationship with her father?

Themes

Because of Winn-Dixie is one of those stories that 'restore faith in humanity.' This gentle story involves a lot of compassion, sympathy, and forgiveness. One of the most heartwarming processes throughout the book was Opal learning how to accept and understand Otis. Otis is an ex-criminal: he has been to prison for accidentally punching a cop. Keyword: *accidentally*. We all have moments when we get excessively annoyed by something or somebody. And in those moments of heat, our judgment may temporarily become hazy, and we may lose our composure—the result: an accident. However, even if it was an *accident*, what's done is done, and one needs to own up to their mistake. Being "in heat" or "in distress" can *never* be an excuse for committing a crime. Otis served his time in jail, during which he realized and accepted his mistakes. This doesn't erase his past, however—he will forever carry the crime on his record. Yet this also doesn't make him entirely an evil person—he has had his awakening and is trying his best to make amends. Would you say that Otis deserves forgiveness? What about his crime? Should he be continuously tagged for what he's done in the past? If former criminals behave themselves in the present, does that lift their past misdemeanor from their reputation? How about Gloria and her problems with alcohol in the past? How about Opal's father failing to keep his ex-wife from leaving the family? Do they deserve forgiveness?

Friendship is another crucial aspect of this book. Every friend Opal makes benefits considerably from their friendship (and so does Opal). All of them were alone and lonely before becoming friends with Opal. Some people enjoy solitude, but this doesn't mean these people never get lonely. When left alone, people tend to obsess over their past mistakes and embarrassing moments. Reflection is mandatory, but *excessive* reflection may damage you instead. Having understanding friends with who you can share your scars can heal you incredibly. We witness this from all the characters who become friends with each other—Otis, Miss Franny, Gloria Dump, the preacher, and even Opal herself. Each of them has their own unique wound deep down in their mind—Miss Franny has one about her great-grandfather Littmus W. Block, Gloria has one about her past relationship with alcohol, Otis has one about being in jail, and so on. By sharing these painful memories, the characters heal and recover. The power of friends, am I right?

The book also puts ten cents into *how you make friends*. Have you ever had the experience of *accidentally* becoming friends with someone? It is often not easy to lower your guard against strangers and treat them as if you've known them for years. However, it's also not a good idea to be adamantly defensive whenever you meet new people. Sometimes, *honest mistakes* could precipitate you to get close to others. It could also allow others to view you as someone approachable and down-to-earth. Try being open and relaxed—you'll find yourself making new friends left and right.

1 Summary and First Impressions

A. Can you give a short summary of the story?

B. What do you think about the story? Do you like it?

C. If you saw a stray dog or a cat that looked like it needed help, would you take it in? Why, or why would you not?

2 Story Questions

A. Who does Opal meet at the Winn-Dixie grocery store? What was he doing there? Why does Opal announce that he's her dog, and what name does she give him?

B. How does Opal describe the condition of Winn-Dixie when she first met him? Was he in good shape?

C. What did Opal's father tell her about her mother (the ten facts), especially about their marriage and her issue with alcohol?

D. Who is the first friend Opal makes in Naomi? What is her job? How was Winn-Dixie involved in the two becoming friends?

E. How did Miss Franny Block get to own a library? Retell the story about her encounter with the bear.

F. What did Opal want to purchase at Gertrude's Pets? Why did she offer to work for Otis? How was Winn-Dixie involved in Opal getting her job?

G. Who is the next friend Opal makes in Naomi? How was Winn-Dixie involved in the two becoming friends? What does she feed to Winn-Dixie and Opal, and what does Opal do in her garden?

H. What did Opal find Otis doing for the animals in the pet store when she arrived at work one day? What did he say about his behavior and about his past?

I. How was the tree in Gloria's backyard decorated? What did Gloria say about the decorations and her relationship with alcohol in the past? What did she say about Otis?

J. Retell the story of Miss Franny's great-grandfather, Littmus W. Block. Why did he decide to manufacture candies? What was his candies called? What special flavor did his candies have, and why?

K. Why had Otis been to jail in the past? On what account was he released from jail?

L. What happens to Winn-Dixie during the party in Gloria's garden? What does Opal learn about her mother while searching for Winn-Dixie with her father? Where was Winn-Dixie all the time?

③ Character Questions

A. Why does Opal feel lonely at the start of the story? Why does she call her father "the preacher"?

B. Why had Opal's mother left her husband? Does the preacher still think about his ex-wife? Why does he preach so hard?

C. What does Opal learn about living with sorrow from Miss Franny Block's story about her great-grandfather?

D. What does Opal learn from Otis about people that have been to jail? What does Gloria tell her about Otis?

E. What lessons did Gloria teach Opal? What did she say about patience, alcohol, and parting with someone?

F. How was Winn-Dixie able to connect with all of Opal's new friends? What did he share with each of them (i.e., Miss Franny, Otis, and Gloria)?

④ Theme Questions

A. Otis is a noteworthy character in the book. Like many of us, Opal considered ex-convicts as dangerous people. Hence, when she first heard that Otis had been to jail, she was shocked. However, what shocked her even more was how nice and sincere Otis was now. Opal expected ex-criminals to be vicious and aggressive, but Otis was quite the opposite. When Opal opened up about her confusion about Otis to Gloria, she told her an important lesson: that even nice people could have done incorrect things in the past. Gloria says that everybody makes mistakes and we should not judge people solely based on their past.

What do you think about ex-criminals? Do you think they realize and regret their mistakes? Do you think ex-criminals can change?

B. In the story, Winn-Dixie seems to express plenty of affection to the people around him. Winn-Dixie never fails to comfort or cheer up people. At the same time, Winn-Dixie also seems to understand that people equally love him back. Though he may not comprehend the language, he seems to firmly grasp that he is being loved.

Do you think pets can be affectionate toward humans? Do you think pets can, in a way, understand what humans tell them?

Vocabulary Exercise

Instructions

These are some words and phrases used in *Because of Winn-Dixie*. Write each of their definition in English. Then, for each word, create your own sentence including that word. Be mindful that one word can have multiple meanings or be used in more than one way. Carefully consider how the words and phrases were used in the original book, and try to use each word/phrase the same way as how the book used it.

Words & Phrases

memorize	introduce	invent	by accident	pay attention to
absolutely	convince	advanced (*adj.*)	all of a sudden	can't help (but)

Sentences from the book

Here are the sentences from the original book that contains the given words and phrases. Only use these as reference and do not write the same sentences for your exercise.

memorize: I **memorized** it the same way I had **memorized** the list of ten things about my mama.

introduce: Before he could run away, I **introduced** him to the preacher.

invent: "It's some candy Miss Franny's great-grandfather **invented**."

by accident & all of a sudden: … like it's all happening **by accident**, like he doesn't intent to get on the couch, but **all of a sudden**, there he is.

pay attention to: He didn't **pay** any **attention to** me.

absolutely: … and wagged his tail something furious; so I knew he **absolutely** loved that leash and collar combination.

convince: After I got Otis **convinced** to come, the rest of getting ready for the party was easy and fun.

advanced (*adj.*): "I would like something even more difficult to read now, because I am an

advanced reader."

can't help (but): But I **couldn't help** it. I couldn't let that dog go to the pound.

Paragraph Write-up Exercise

Instructions

Write a short paragraph expressing your thoughts about the following questions. There are multiple questions to guide you arrange your thoughts and form your answer. Be sure to answer all the questions within a single paragraph—do not answer the questions individually.

A "paragraph" is a collection of sentences (which are not divided into separate lines) that convey a single idea throughout. The sentences in a paragraph must be logically arranged to coherently deliver your thoughts to the reader. A single paragraph must contain at least three sentences.

Question

Do you think people who do nice things in the present, but have done wrong things in the past (e.g., ex-criminals) must be treated nicely? Do you think these people know what they've done is wrong and accept their mistakes?

Bibliography

About the Author

Katrina "Kate" Elizabeth DiCamillo (58; born Mar 25, 1964) is an American children and young adults' author born in Pennsylvania, U.S. She often writes about young protagonists who overcome loneliness and become independent. Her most well-known works include *Because of Winn-Dixie*, *Flora & Ulysses: The Illuminated Adventures*, and *The Tale of Despereaux*.

https://www.katedicamillo.com/

Other Books by the Author

Columns of each table: (from left) Title of Book; Year Published; ATOS Book Level; Lexile Measure; Interest Level.

Guide to Interest Level:

LG (Lower Grades; suitable for grades K-3)

MG (Middle Grades; suitable for grades 4-8)

MG+ (Middle Grades Plus; suitable for grades 6+)

UG (Upper Grades; suitable for grades 9-12)

Early Chapter Books				
Tales from Deckawoo Drive (6 Books)	2014-2020	3.7-3.8	430L-570L	LG
Mercy Watson (6 Books)	2005-2009	2.6-3.2	450L-550L	LG
Bink & Gollie (3 Books)	2010-2013	2.2-2.7	450L-570L	LG

Three Rancheros				
Raymie Nightingale	2016	4.2	550L	MG
Louisiana's Way Home	2018	4.5	630L	MG
Beverly, Right Here	2019	3.5	480L	MG

Novels				
Because of Winn-Dixie **2001 Newbery Honor	2000	3.9	670L	MG
The Tiger Rising	2001	4.0	590L	MG
The Tale of Despereaux *2004 Newbery Medal	2003	4.7	670L	MG
The Miraculous Journey of Edward Tulane	2006	4.4	700L	MG
The Magician's Elephant	2009	5.0	730L	MG
Flora and Ulysses *2014 Newbery Medal	2012	4.3	520L	MG
The Beatryce Prophecy	2021	4.4		MG

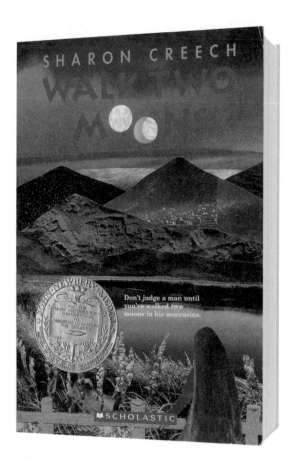

Walk Two Moons

by Sharon Creech

Published	1994 (1995 Newbery Medal)
ATOS Book Level	4.9
Lexile	770L
Word Count	59400

Plot Introduction

Don't judge a man until you've walked two moons in his moccasins.
— Cheyenne (Native American) Proverb

Every person is complex—an individual is comprised of convoluted experiences and sophisticated emotions. To thoroughly understand one, you'd need to walk at least *two moons* in their shoes. Our heroine, Salamanca "Sal" Tree Hiddle, learns this by heart as she recounts her best friend Phoebe's fascinating story. As the book begins, Sal embarks on a journey to meet her mother. Sal's mother left home a while ago, saying she wants some time alone. It has been weeks, but she is yet to return. The trip is *ambitious*: they must travel from Euclid, Ohio, to Lewiston, Idaho—practically across the entire continent. To ease the pain of the extended road trip, Sal tells the story of her friend, Phoebe Winterbottom. Around a year ago, Sal and her father recently moved from their hometown, Bybanks, Kentucky, to Euclid, Ohio. This was so her father could be closer to a woman called Margaret Cadaver. Sal suspects her father is abandoning her mom, and she is disgruntled. The move *does* bring Sal some righteousness, though, as she befriends a bright, imaginative girl: Phoebe. Sal describes Phoebe's family to be highly mannered and respectable. However, it seems Phoebe's mother, Mrs. Winterbottom, doesn't adjust to this system well. She is also frustrated about how nobody appreciates all she provides for the family. One day, a mysterious man visits Phoebe's house and asks for Mrs. Winterbottom, who was absent at the moment. Soon after the visit, Phoebe's mother leaves home, saying she needs some time alone. She later returns as a totally changed person, accompanied by the mysterious visitor, and his shocking identity is revealed. As Sal tells Phoebe's story, she begins to comprehend why *her mother* had to leave. Will Sal safely reach Lewiston and reunite with her mother?

Themes

My job is merely to introduce the book, but I strongly urge you to read this yourself—it is truly a masterpiece. All the nuances, all the hints, all the twists and turns—you've got to experience them *firsthand* by reading the actual book yourself. Accordingly, beware that this section contains critical spoilers on the plot.

The title, the related proverb (that I've written above), and the whole story all howl the main theme of this book: *empathy*. As Sal tells the story of Mrs. Winterbottom, she tries to position herself "in Mrs. Winterbottom's moccasins." By doing so, she comprehends not only Mrs. Winterbottom's actions but also *her mother's* actions in the past. For every event related to Mrs. Winterbottom Sal recounts, she begins to fathom why her mother behaved in particular ways, which emotions she would have felt, and why she ultimately had left. Likewise, discovering why she was angry with Phoebe makes her wonder if her father ever felt the same way toward her for the same reasons. (Sal's father became uptight and sensitive toward Sal after his wife had left.) With all this practice, Sal tenderly empathizes with Mrs. Cadaver on her husband's death. She also realizes how childish her suspicion about her father's genuine friend was. Sal's empathy and maturity shine again as she grieves Gram's death with Gramps. Recalling the past, putting herself in others' moccasins, and developing the ability to empathize, Sal truly grows up.

There's a constructive activity you should try based on the story. Of all the wonderful tales offered in *Walk Two Moons*, the accounts of Mrs. Winterbottom and Sal's mother, Chanhassen Hiddle, are amusingly similar. Specifically, their stories involve the following identical key points.

- Each of them identifies the desirable "ideal mother" portrait and gets frustrated after realizing they're incapable of achieving it despite their efforts.

- Each of them loses their grip on their identity.

- Each of them becomes isolated/alienated from their family.

- Each of them experiences a "critical event" that gives them the epiphany which prompts them to leave their home.

It's definitely a worthwhile exercise to arrange relevant events from the book under the above four criteria. You may have to work through the story multiple times, focusing on Mrs. Winterbottom's narrative once and Mrs. Hiddle's the next. Exploring from both characters' perspectives will enlighten you on the entire story and reveal the book's message about *finding yourself*. Below, I provide a rough guide to get you going; try to expand on the explanations by determining the relevant parts of the story.

	Mrs. Winterbottom	Mrs. Hiddle
What is the "ideal mother figure" for each of them?	Stay-at-home mom who always stays on top of all the chores around the house (e.g., cooking, cleaning, laundry, and taking care of the children).	One who can fill the house with children (i.e., one who can give birth to and take care of many children).
Why do they lose their own identities?	Mr. Winterbottom is too strict and proper for her; Mrs. Winterbottom tries to be someone she's not.	Mrs. Hiddle is too fixated on becoming an excellent mother—giving birth to many and perfecting her housekeeping skills.
Why do they become alienated from their families?	No one appreciates all the work Mrs. Winterbottom does around the house.	Mr. Hiddle is too nice to Mrs. Hiddle and Sal; Mrs. Hiddle worries she may never be able to reciprocate the same amount of love.
Which critical events happened for them to decide to leave their houses?	A long-lost family member visits her home.	Endures a miscarriage and a hysterectomy.

Unlike most books, which have one or two main theme(s) and a few extra minor ones, this book contains several notable bite-sized topics. The first relates to *your emotions*. After Mrs. Hiddle's departure, Sal felt obligated to feel sad and continue to do so. One day, she observes a newborn calf struggling to stand up, which cracks her up. She then realizes she doesn't *have to* feel sad all the time. She learns that there's no emotion a person is *supposed to* feel; there's only the emotion that one feels *at a given moment*.

The book also discusses *holding grudges*. At the start, Sal is angry at both her parents—her mother for leaving home and her father for not stopping her. As Sal refuses to forgive her mother, she is unable to move on from the loss, and as Sal refuses to forgive her father, her family spirals deeper into depression. Toward the end of the story, thankfully, Sal lets go of her grudges. This allows her to recover from her mother's departure and restore her relationship with her father.

Death is another idea the book highlights. There are many deaths in the book—Gram, Mrs. Cadaver's husband, and more. Through all the unfortunate losses, perhaps the book's trying to say that *death happens*. It is sad and certainly not easy to deal with, but we can't delay or deny it forever. We need to learn to accept and cope with loss.

Questions

① Summary and First Impressions

A. Can you give a short summary of the story?

B. What do you think about the story? Do you like it?

C. Do you know anybody around you whose parents left their house? Why did they leave, and did they ever come back?

② Story Questions

A. What is the relationship between Mrs. Cadaver and Sal's father? (How does he know her?) Why is Sal not happy about Mrs. Cadaver at first?

B. Why did Sal's father adore Mrs. Cadaver so much? Did he still miss his old wife, Chanhassen?

C. How do the Winterbottoms behave? How is Mrs. Winterbottom (i.e., Phoebe's mother) treated at home by her family? How does she feel about herself?

D. Who came to Phoebe's house while she and Sal were at home by themselves? What did he ask them, and how did Phoebe think about him?

E. From the next day, what kept appearing at the porch of the Winterbottom house? Who did Phoebe thought was leaving the notes, and who was actually leaving the notes? Why did the person leave the notes?

F. What happens to Gram as they go swimming in Missouri River? What did Tom Fleet and Gramps do to help her? When did she recover?

G. What does Phoebe think had happened to her mother? What does she do to prove this?

H. What events had happened leading up to Sal's mother leaving her house back in Bybanks?

I. To whom does Phoebe take the evidence she had collected to? How did the person react? What happened to the kids?

J. On Phoebe and Sal's second visit to Sergeant Bickle, what does Sal discover about the "lunatic"?

K. How do Sal and Phoebe track down where the lunatic is? What do they witness when they visit where he is staying?

L. Who did Mrs. Winterbottom bring with her as she returned home? Who was the person that accompanied her (i.e., what was their identity)? What was Mr. Winterbottom's reaction to this?

M. What did Sal learn about Margaret Cadaver that day? How had she met her father?

N. Who does Sal meet while going down the Lewiston Hill? How does the person help Sal?

③ Character Questions

A. Is Sal empathetic? Does her empathy toward others grow as the story continues?

B. How does Sal's attitude toward Mrs. Cadaver change throughout the story? Why does it change so? How about her attitude toward her mother, does it also change?

C. How are Phoebe's personalities? What's special about her?

D. Sal regularly comments on how ridiculous Phoebe's imaginations can be. Still, they remain as great friends. How can Sal and Phoebe be so compatible with each other?

④ Theme Questions

A. Throughout the book, Sal gains a great deal of understanding toward her mother's departure by telling a very similar story—that of Mrs. Winterbottom's. Before, Sal deeply resented her mother and never tried to recognize the emotions her mother would have felt. However, as she tells Mrs. Winterbottom's story to her grandparents, she starts to comprehend many parts about her own mother's leaving.

Do you think comparing events that happened in the distant past with more recent events can grant you further understanding about the older events? Have you ever had such an experience yourself?

B. As stated above, Sal starts understanding all the details related to her mother's departure only after she observes it from an objective (third-person) perspective. Do you think an event is much easier to understand when you are not directly involved? What do you think about the proverb: "Don't judge a man until you've walked two moons in his moccasins?"

Vocabulary Exercise

Instructions

These are some words and phrases used in *Walk Two Moons*. Write each of their definition in English. Then, for each word, create your own sentence including that word. Be mindful that one word can have multiple meanings or be used in more than one way. Carefully consider how the words and phrases were used in the original book, and try to use each word/phrase the same way as how the book used it.

Words & Phrases

occasionally	impression	peculiar	vivid
temporarily	potential	suspect	evidence
fill [*n.*] (up) to the brim		it (has/had) occurred to me that	

Sentences from the book

Here are the sentences from the original book that contains the given words and phrases. Only use these as reference and do not write the same sentences for your exercise.

occasionally: But, **occasionally**, in small, unexpected moments, the corners of my other's mouth would turn down and she'd say, "Really? Is that so?" and sound exactly like a Pickford.

impression: Even though she had a pleasant, round face and long, curly yellow hair, the main **impression** I got was that she was used to being plain and ordinary …

peculiar: It all seemed **peculiar**. They acted to thumpingly *tidy* and *respectable*.

vivid: Like I said, she has a **vivid** imagination.

temporarily: … and that Ben was living with Mary Lou's family **temporarily**.

potential: Then Phoebe told her mother about the **potential** lunatic who had come to the house earlier.

suspect: Ever since my mother left us that April day, I **suspected** that everyone was going to leave, one by one.

evidence: "I'm going to search for clues, for **evidence** that the lunatic has been here and dragged my mother off."

fill [n.] (up) to the brim: "We'll fill the house up with children! We'll **fill it** right **up to the brim!**

It (has/had) occurred to me that: **It occurred to me that** my father didn't hug me as much anymore.

Paragraph Write-up Exercise

Instructions

Write a short paragraph expressing your thoughts about the following questions. There are multiple questions to guide you arrange your thoughts and form your answer. Be sure to answer all the questions within a single paragraph—do not answer the questions individually.

A "paragraph" is a collection of sentences (which are not divided into separate lines) that convey a single idea throughout. The sentences in a paragraph must be logically arranged to coherently deliver your thoughts to the reader. A single paragraph must contain at least three sentences.

Question

Normal: What would it be like if your mother had left your family? How would your father and you (and your siblings, if you have any) feel? How would your daily routine change?

Challenge: How are the stories of Mrs. Winterbottom and Sal's mother similar? Why did they feel like they were losing their identities? Why did they feel alienated from their families? Which critical events occurred for them to decide to leave their houses? Do you think Sal's mother would have eventually returned home if she hadn't died so soon?

Bibliography

About the Author

Sharon Creech (77; born July 29, 1945) is an American children and young adults' author born in Ohio, U.S. She tackles serious topics such as independence, trust, adulthood, and death in her novels. Her most well-known works include *Walk Two Moons* and *Ruby Holler*.

https://www.sharoncreech.com/

Other Books by the Author

Columns of each table: (from left) Title of Book; Year Published; ATOS Book Level; Lexile Measure; Interest Level.

Guide to Interest Level:

LG (Lower Grades; suitable for grades K-3)

MG (Middle Grades; suitable for grades 4-8)

MG+ (Middle Grades Plus; suitable for grades 6+)

UG (Upper Grades; suitable for grades 9-12)

Sharon Creech Narrative Poetry Series				
Love That Dog	2001	4.5	1010L	MG
Hate That Cat	2008	5.0	NP	MG
Moo	2016	4.4	790L	MG

Novels				
Absolutely Normal Chaos	1990	4.7	840L	MG
Walk Two Moons *1995 Newbery Medal	1994	4.9	770L	MG
Pleasing the Ghost	1996	3.0	520L	MG
Chasing Redbird	1997	5.0	790L	MG
Bloomability	1998	5.2	850L	MG
The Wanderer *2001 Newbery Honor	2000	5.2	830L	MG
Ruby Holler *2003 Carnegie Medal	2002	4.3	660L	MG
Granny Torrelli Makes Soup	2003	4.2	810L	MG
Heartbeat	2004	5.0	NP	MG
Replay	2005	4.2	780L	MG
The Castle Corona	2007	5.5	800L	MG
The Unfinished Angel	2009	4.4	810L	MG
The Great Unexpected	2012	4.3	720L	MG
The Boy on the Porch	2013	4.0	680L	MG
Saving Winslow	2018	4.2	690L	MG
One Time	2020	4.8		MG

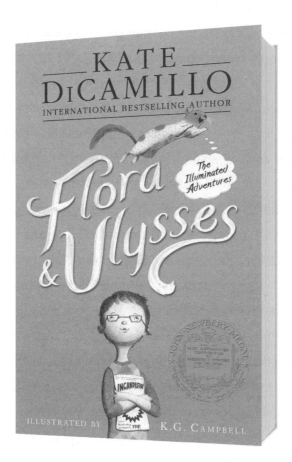

Flora & Ulysses

by Kate DiCamillo

Published	2013 (2014 Newbery Medal)
ATOS Book Level	4.3
Lexile	520L
Word Count	32790

Plot Introduction

Have you ever sucked a bug into a vacuum cleaner? What would happen to the bug? Something as small would probably not survive the power of a vacuum. But what if you sucked in a *squirrel* instead? Well, according to *Flora and Ulysses*, the squirrel will gain superpowers. Ulysses was merely a helpless little squirrel before he was swallowed by Mrs. Tootie's ultrapowerful vacuum. Surprise, surprise: out he comes with the ability to fly, lift things hundreds of times heavier than him, and comprehend English. Flora, Mrs. Tootie's neighbor (and today's heroine), has always wished for a superhero to appear in her life, and she is elated by Ulysses's transformation. She brings the squirrel home, but her novelist mother, Phyllis, is not pleased—to her, Ulysses is nothing but a dirty, germ-spreading wild animal. She even asks her ex-husband, George, to "take care of" Ulysses, handing him a shovel. (Thankfully, he refuses to deliver her request.) Flora, her father, and Ulysses head to a local diner, where chaos ensues—Ulysses accidentally lands in the waitress's hair, then flies around the restaurant until he injures himself by diving headfirst into a glass door. Flora takes him to Dr. Meescham, who lives in the same building as her dad. It turns out Dr. Meescham is not *that* kind of doctor (she is a doctor of philosophy), but she helps Ulysses recover anyway. The next day, the three return to Phyllis's place, where Ulysses gets caught red-handed using Phyllis's typewriter (which she adores). Phyllis decides she's had enough and attempts to eliminate Ulysses once and for all. Fortunately, Ulysses escapes from Phyllis's grasp. After realizing Ulysses has disappeared, Flora sets out to search for Ulysses. Will Flora be able to reunite with her superhero?

Themes

What makes one a superhero? Being able to fly? To turn invisible? To lift things hundreds of times heavier than one's body? Not always. Even those without any superpowers can become superheroes. What does it take, then? Perhaps a good place to begin is the *mindset*. To be a superhero, you must establish the mentality to willingly sacrifice yourself and risk your life to save others. A true superhero acts before thinking in the case of an emergency; for them, the health of others is paramount. Without a doubt, it is challenging even to develop such a mindset, let alone preserve it in the most dangerous times. The point is: you *do not* need superpowers to become a superhero. Think of the people around you—there are already countless superheroes among us! Who are they? For starters: the police officers, the firefighters, and the like. These people continuously sacrifice their time and effort—and sometimes even their lives—to ensure the safety of our lives. If these are "universal" superheroes, everyone also has "personalized" superheroes that focus on your safety alone—your parents. Your parents are superheroes who will endure perilous adversities to keep you safe. Who else do you think are superheroes? Who else—alive or dead—would be worthy of the title?

A minor theme of this book is *love*—especially *family love*. In the beginning, Flora is unsure if anybody loves her—her father is away, her mother doesn't care about her enough, and it appears she is the only child. But, as the story continues, Flora makes amends with her father and develops a proper father-daughter relationship. In addition, she realizes that her mother *does* love her; she's just not versed in expressing her emotions. Phyllis appears to remain indifferent toward her daughter's actions throughout the book, but it turns out that she was genuinely concerned about her beloved daughter all along. Even her hate towards Ulysses stemmed from her genuine worry toward Flora (that she may never seek to make "normal, i.e., human, friends").

Questions

① Summary and First Impressions

A. Can you describe your favorite part of the story? Why do you like the part the most?

B. What do you think about the story? Do you like it?

② Discussion Questions

A. What do you think would happen to a squirrel if it was actually sucked up into a vacuum cleaner? Do you think it would die? If not, how do you think it would be different when you take it out of the vacuum? Would there be any difference?

B. Why do you think the author chose a squirrel to be a superhero? Could it be because squirrels are inherently small and frail? Would you ever expect a squirrel to be a superhero? Could there be other reasons for this choice?

> ### Chew on this
>
> "So my mom had a vacuum cleaner that she loved, and she passed away in 2009. In the last year of her life, she kept on saying 'what's going to happen to the vacuum cleaner when I'm gone?' And I was like, 'why are we worried about the vacuum cleaner? There are bigger things to worry about,' but when she died, I did as I promised her I would do. I took the vacuum cleaner so that it would have a good home …
> Then, the spring after my mother died, there was a squirrel on the front steps of my house, draped dramatically across the steps, clearly in distress. And he wouldn't move when I got close to him, and I didn't know what to do for him. I called my best friend who lives a block away and said 'help me, there's a squirrel dying on my front steps.' … she said 'get the t-shirt, get the shovel, I will come over there and whack him over the head.' … I thought about ways to save the squirrel's life and I combined it with the vacuum cleaner … Well, the squirrel left when he heard my friend saying 'whack him over the head with a shovel.' You know, the squirrel was like 'I'm no dummy.'"
> - **Disney+ Press Conference for Flora & Ulysses** (movie based on the book), **Feb 9, 2021.**

C. Why do you think Flora's mother hated and mistreated Ulysses so much throughout the story? Do you think Ulysses made her worry that her daughter might never look to make human friends? Do you think Phyllis just hated wild squirrels? What other reasons do you think were there?

D. Flora's mother was worried that, because of Ulysses, Flora may not work on making human friends. Do you think everybody needs human friends? Is a pet not enough?

    i.   What can a human friend do for us that a pet cannot?

    ii.   What can a pet do for us that a human friend cannot?

E. Why do you think William Spiver was (or pretended to be) blind? What do you think about the story of his stepfather? Would you be as distressed as William Spiver?

> ### Reminder
>
> William wanted to be addressed specifically as "William Spiver" so he could have the same name as his biological father, William, yet would be distinguished (because of the additional part, "Spiver"). His stepfather, Tyrone, called him Billy "one time too many," which "cracked" William, who pushed his truck into a lake. When William's mother found out, she got furious and sent him to live with his grandmother, Mrs. Tootie.

F. What would you say is the most heroic act that Ulysses displayed throughout the book? Would you say that Ulysses is indeed a superhero?

G. Why do you think Flora's parents got divorced in the first place? How were they able to get back together so easily at the end of the story?

H. Why do you think Flora went to get help from William Spiver and Tootie when she found out that Ulysses went missing? Why didn't she go searching for him on her own? Why didn't she ask someone else?

I. Do you like superheroes? Who is your favorite superhero?

J. If you could be a superhero, what would be your superpowers? Who would be your arch-nemesis?

K. What does it take to be a superhero? Can people with no superpowers become superheroes too? Who do you think is closest to being a superhero near you?

Vocabulary Exercise

Instructions

These are some words and phrases used in *Flora and Ulysses*. Write each of their definition in English. Then, write a paragraph with the topic of your liking using <u>at least seven</u> of these words/phrases. Be mindful that one word/phrase can have multiple meanings or be used in more than one way. Carefully consider how the words and phrases were used in the original book, and try to use each word/phrase the same way as how the book used it.

Words & Phrases

beloved	appalled	glance	exhilarating	outrage (*v.* or *n.*)
soothing	influence	undeniable	unnecessarily	professional (*adj.* or *n.*)

Sentences from the book

Here are the sentences from the original book that contains the given words and phrases. Only use these as reference and do not write the same sentences for your exercise.

beloved: "Yes, you. Little flower. Flora Belle. **Beloved** of your father, MR. George Buckman …"

appalled: Basically, Tootie drove with one finger on the wheel. Flora's father would have been **appalled**.

glance: "What are you doing?" her mother said to Flora … "Oh, nothing," said Flora. She **glanced** at the squirrel in her arms.

exhilarating: They were speeding down the road. It was alarming and **exhilarating** to be going so fast.

outrage: "Talking to my baby doll?" said Flora. She felt a flush of **outrage** crawl up her cheeks. For the love of Pete! She was ten years old, almost eleven.

soothing: "It will all take just a minute," said Tootie in a low, **soothing** voice.

influence: It was dangerous to allow yourself to believe that what you said directly **influenced** the universe.

undeniable: Flora was certain that this was a true and genuine emergency, an absolute and **undeniable** crime.

unnecessarily: "… perhaps you would like to retract those last words? They seem **unnecessarily** harsh."

professional: "What goes on here is a serious business," said her mother. "I am a **professional** writer …"

Paragraph Write-up Exercise

Instructions

Write a short paragraph expressing your thoughts about the following questions. There are multiple questions to guide you arrange your thoughts and form your answer. Be sure to answer all the questions within a single paragraph—do not answer the questions individually.

A "paragraph" is a collection of sentences (which are not divided into separate lines) that convey a single idea throughout. The sentences in a paragraph must be logically arranged to coherently deliver your thoughts to the reader. A single paragraph must contain at least three sentences.

Question

Among all the people you know (people around you, historical icons, famous people that are alive now, etc.) who do you think is the closest to being a superhero? Why?

Bibliography

1 – "Disney+ Press 'Conference: "Flora & Ulysses"" from *AllEars.Net*
(https://allears.net/2021/02/19/disney-press-conference-flora-ulysses/)

About the Author

Katrina "Kate" Elizabeth DiCamillo (58; born Mar 25, 1964) is an American children and young adults' author born in Pennsylvania, U.S. She often writes about young protagonists who overcome loneliness and become independent. Her most well-known works include *Because of Winn-Dixie*, *Flora & Ulysses: The Illuminated Adventures*, and *The Tale of Despereaux*.

https://www.katedicamillo.com/

Other Books by the Author

Columns of each table: (from left) Title of Book; Year Published; ATOS Book Level; Lexile Measure; Interest Level.

Guide to Interest Level:

LG (Lower Grades; suitable for grades K-3)

MG (Middle Grades; suitable for grades 4-8)

MG+ (Middle Grades Plus; suitable for grades 6+)

UG (Upper Grades; suitable for grades 9-12)

Early Chapter Books				
Tales from Deckawoo Drive (6 Books)	2014-2020	3.7-3.8	430L-570L	LG
Mercy Watson (6 Books)	2005-2009	2.6-3.2	450L-550L	LG
Bink & Gollie (3 Books)	2010-2013	2.2-2.7	450L-570L	LG

Three Rancheros				
Raymie Nightingale	2016	4.2	550L	MG
Louisiana's Way Home	2018	4.5	630L	MG
Beverly, Right Here	2019	3.5	480L	MG

Novels				
Because of Winn-Dixie **2001 Newbery Honor	2000	3.9	670L	MG
The Tiger Rising	2001	4.0	590L	MG
The Tale of Despereaux *2004 Newbery Medal	2003	4.7	670L	MG
The Miraculous Journey of Edward Tulane	2006	4.4	700L	MG
The Magician's Elephant	2009	5.0	730L	MG
Flora and Ulysses *2014 Newbery Medal	2012	4.3	520L	MG
The Beatryce Prophecy	2021	4.4		MG

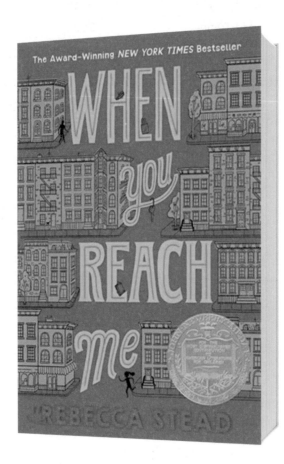

When You Reach Me

by Rebecca Stead

Published	2009 (2010 Newbery Medal)
ATOS Book Level	4.5
Lexile	750L
Word Count	39253

Plot Introduction

Here's a little memory game: do you remember *A Wrinkle in Time*? Well, if you enjoyed that book, you're on the same page as Rebecca Stead, the author of this book. Inspired by Madeline L'Engle's masterpiece, *When You Reach Me* presents a delicious mystery rooted in time travel. The thriller is hinted right at the beginning as Miranda, our heroine, introduces an obscure character: "the Laughing Man"—a homeless man who lives under the mailbox outside Miranda's apartment. Meanwhile, Miranda has been having some relationship troubles with her dearest friend, Sal—he decided to suddenly distance himself from Miranda after getting punched by Marcus, an unfamiliar boy in Miranda's school. Unlike his initial hostility, Marcus turns out to be an ordinary kid; Miranda befriends him after having a conversation over her favorite book: (you've guessed it!) *A Wrinkle in Time* at the school dentist's office. At this point, Miranda starts receiving weird, creepy notes from an unknown person. In one of them, the sender claims that he arrived from the future to save Miranda's friend and asks her to write a letter about *things that haven't happened yet*. Another one even *predicts* several events that hadn't happened yet! While Miranda attempts to decipher these bizarre notes, Sal almost gets hit by a truck. Inches before contact, an unlikely yet familiar face appears out of nowhere and kicks Sal out of the way, sacrificing his life and saving Sal's. Finally, Miranda gets face to face with who was sending the cryptic notes. Then, Miranda begins to comprehend. She soon realizes who the savior truly is and that he is not far away from her. She knows exactly who to write to and what. Read the book yourself to find out the answer to this compelling riddle!

Themes

If *this* isn't a book that makes you think about *time travel*, then I don't know what is. Throughout the book, there are several instances when Marcus and Miranda (and, optionally, Julia) discuss the technicalities of time travel. (Well, if you can call them "discussions" because most of the arguing comes from Marcus.) Of the many perplexing elements of time travel, the book focuses on the debate: "Can *two of you* exist in the *same timeline*?" Let's say that you've traveled *back* in time; what happens to you in the *departure timeline* (i.e., the *future*, where you came from)? Do you disappear? Is there no "you" in the departure timeline anymore? What about the *arrival timeline*? Do *two of you* exist at the same time now? (The older you from the future and the younger you who was already living in the past?) What happens if the two of you meet? Is it possible? Is one of you going to die? All these questions are probably questions you've never considered before because you probably don't care *this* much about time travel—but they're still fascinating, aren't they? At the end of the day, it depends on how you conceive time travel—are you messing with time in your own world (i.e., from your point of view), or are you crossing over to another timeline (perhaps a parallel universe)?

Like some other books, this book has a single main theme and not many other discernable ones. There's a little hint at *family dynamics*, as we see that Miranda's biological father is missing, but the book doesn't take that idea much further. There's also a little about *friendship*, as Miranda has some difficulties with Sal, but the book doesn't take this much further either—why Sal decided to distance himself from Miranda is never explained in full. He states that he wanted to hang out with some other friends (especially male friends)—and we can also guess that it must have been awfully embarrassing to get plummeted to the ground by Marcus in front of Miranda—but the book doesn't make a big deal out of this. There's also something about *racism*, as Julia, a black girl, is looked down upon by Jimmy, the infamous sandwich shop owner. However, in the end, nothing's particularly more important than *time* and *time travel* when it comes to *When You Reach Me*.

Questions

① Summary and First Impressions

A. Can you describe your favorite part of the story? Why do you like the part the most?

B. What do you think about the story? Do you like it?

② Discussion Questions

A. Now that you've read the book, what do you think about the ending of *A Wrinkle in Time?* Do you agree with Marcus that the kids should have seen themselves arrive before they left?

> ### *Reminder*
>
> Marcus and Miranda have a discussion about the ending of *A Wrinkle in Time* when they were waiting together at the school dentist's office. Marcus catches Miranda with the book and says that he's unsure about its ending. Marcus argues that: had the kids (i.e., Meg, Calvin, and Charles Wallace) actually arrived on Earth five minutes before they left, they must have seen themselves come back before they ever left. However, since they do not see themselves return at the beginning of the story, he claims that the three Mrs. W's lied to the kids, and they did not return any time before they left.)

B. If you were to travel in time right now, do you think it could be possible for two of you to exist at the same time (with different ages), like Marcus and the Laughing Man?

    i. If yes, what do you think will happen if the two of you? What do you think happens to the "you" in the future timeline (i.e., where you came from)?

    ii. If no, what do you think happens to the "you" in the past timeline (i.e., where you arrived)? Does the young "you" disappear once you arrive?

C. What was your opinion on the Laughing Man before his identity was revealed? Did you think he was an important character? Did you guess that he might be someone else in the book? Did you expect him to be a time traveler?

D. Why do you think Sal decided to distance himself from Miranda after he got punched by Marcus?

> **Reminder**
>
> One day, while Sal and Miranda were walking home from school together, they are confronted by Marcus (who Miranda didn't know the name of at that point). For no apparent reason, Marcus punches Sal in the stomach, who falls to his knees. Marcus nonchalantly leaves the scene, and Sal, after he recovers, darts back home, leaving Miranda behind. After that day, Sal avoids Miranda, and, consequently, Miranda makes new friends and hangs out with them instead.

E. Now that you've completed the book, which of the events that happened in the book was the Laughing Man responsible for? Why do you think so?

F. Why do you think Marcus (the Laughing Man) contacted Miranda when he came back in time from the future? Could he have contacted anyone else?

    i.   What if Marcus contacted himself? What problems do you foresee in that?

    ii.   What if Marcus contacted Sal? What problems do you foresee in that?

    iii.   What if Marcus contacted Julia? What problems do you foresee in that?

G. Why do you think Marcus (the Laughing Man) wrote his notes in such a vague and obscure way? Why do you think he didn't explain in more detail?

    i.   Why do you think Marcus (the Laughing Man) concealed most of the events that would happen in the future even though he already knew all of them?

    ii.   Why do you think Marcus (the Laughing Man) did not reveal his true identity, and, instead, let Miranda figure it out by herself?

H. After comprehending the whole situation, Miranda finishes her letter and hands it over to Marcus (young/current). When or how fast do you think Marcus (young/current) would have realized what Miranda's letter meant? How long do you think it would have taken him to learn the truth?

I. Had Marcus never come back from the future as the Laughing Man, do you think Miranda would have travelled herself to sacrifice her life to save Sal?

Vocabulary Exercise

Instructions

These are some words and phrases used in *When You Reach Me*. Write each of their definition in English. Then, write a paragraph with the topic of your liking using <u>at least seven</u> of these words/phrases. Be mindful that one word/phrase can have multiple meanings or be used in more than one way. Carefully consider how the words and phrases were used in the original book, and try to use each word/phrase the same way as how the book used it.

Words & Phrases

dismiss	pretend	artificial	private	get [*n.*]'s hopes up
distract	reject	appealing (*adj.*)	approve	by any chance

Sentences from the book

Here are the sentences from the original book that contains the given words and phrases. Only use these as reference and do not write the same sentences for your exercise.

dismiss: Sal's class must have been **dismissed** a few minutes before mine—he was walking a little ahead of me.

pretend: It's crazy the things a person can **pretend** not to notice.

artificial: Everything looks **artificial** and kind of gloomy in the dim light.

private: It's like watching someone go through the box of **private** stuff that I keep under my bed.

get [*n.*]'s hopes up: "Don't **get your hopes up**," she warns. "This is just the speed round. The speed round is the easy part."

distract: My second wish was that the laughing man would be gone, or asleep, or at least **distracted** by someone or something else when we walked by.

reject: He had already **rejected** my V-cut for the day …

appealing (*adj.*): … I didn't find those meatballs any more **appealing** than the usual cheese sandwich.

approve: "There's no rush. I just got the plans **approved**. We can start next week …"

by any chance: "… Are you **by any chance** outside, Miranda? It sounds like you might be at a pay phone."

Paragraph Write-up Exercise

Instructions

Write a short paragraph expressing your thoughts about the following questions. There are multiple questions to guide you arrange your thoughts and form your answer. Be sure to answer all the questions within a single paragraph—do not answer the questions individually.

A "paragraph" is a collection of sentences (which are not divided into separate lines) that convey a single idea throughout. The sentences in a paragraph must be logically arranged to coherently deliver your thoughts to the reader. A single paragraph must contain at least three sentences.

Question

If an adult version of you came from the future to meet you right now, what would he/she tell you? How would he/she look like, and what would be his/her job? What questions would you ask your future self?

Bibliography

About the Author

Rebecca Stead (54; born Jan 16, 1968) is an American author born in New York, U.S. Her specialty is mystery-science fiction novels for children and young adults. Her most well-known works include *When You Reach Me* and *Liar & Spy*.

https://rebeccasteadbooks.com/

Other Books by the Author

Columns of each table: (from left) Title of Book; Year Published; ATOS Book Level; Lexile Measure; Interest Level.

Guide to Interest Level:

LG (Lower Grades; suitable for grades K-3)

MG (Middle Grades; suitable for grades 4-8)

MG+ (Middle Grades Plus; suitable for grades 6+)

UG (Upper Grades; suitable for grades 9-12)

Novels				
First Light	2007	4.8	760L	MG
When You Reach Me *2010 Newbery Medal	2009	4.5	750L	MG
Liar & Spy *2014 Carnegie Medal	2012	3.8	670L	MG
Goodbye Stranger	2015	3.9	560L	MG
The List of Things That Will Not Change	2020	4.2	680L	MG

Maniac Magee

by Jerry Spinelli

Published	1990 (1991 Newbery Medal)
ATOS Book Level	4.7
Lexile	820L
Word Count	35427

Two Mills, Pennsylvania gets its name from its territorial layout—the town is divided into two sections: the East End and the West End. But its land is not the only thing that's divided—its *people* are also divided into two: the blacks live in the East End, while the whites live in the West End. What a bizarre scene, isn't it? Our hero today, Jeffery "Maniac" Magee, agrees. Maniac is a white runaway orphan who gets his nickname from his daring stunts. Maniac's legend begins with his reckless act of entering the *East End* (mind you, he's *white*). Perhaps you've guessed it already, but Two Mills is plagued with racism—the whites disparage the blacks, and the blacks despise the whites for this. However, Maniac, who has no idea about racism, happily accepts Mrs. Beale's invitation into her black household in the East End. Thankfully, the Beales consider racism ridiculous, and the entire family welcomes him. Unfortunately, Maniac soon realizes that his black neighbors, unlike the Beales, are *not* pleased. Frustrated, Maniac attempts to turn his reputation around by solving *the Cobble's Knot*—a notorious knot many have failed to untie. With his supreme perseverance, Maniac succeeds in solving the knot, only to find out that it would make no difference. Maniac runs away from the Beale house and heads to the West End; he arrives at the McNab house. There, Manic gathers that the oh-so-great whites are actually *not* so great as they praise themselves. Notwithstanding his disappointment, Maniac attempts once again to resolve racism in Two Mills by inviting Mars Bar, his black friend from the East End, over to a birthday party at the McNab house. Sadly, the party ends in chaos. Will Maniac figure out a decisive way to resolve racism in Two Mills?

Here's an easy question: What do you think is the main theme of this book? That's right: *racism*. "Race" refers to the categorization of people via their physical or social qualities. A person is classified as a particular race based on their looks, social/cultural background, and origin. Humans are often divided into *five* races: African, European, Asian, Oceanian, and Native American. One thing to note here is that modern science considers race practically *meaningless*—with our ancestors having migrated all over the place and our gene pools having mixed aggressively, it's somewhat irrational to divide humans into discrete groups.

Unfortunately, this doesn't scare away *racism*: discrimination of people based on their race. Racism usually works from one race to another—a particular group of people exerts hate on another group of people. The critical point about racism is that it is *baseless* and *habitual*. Racism offers no sensible reason—the hate is systematized and passed down through generations. Yet racism is often nailed deeply within the culture and persists for decades. And that's why racism is absurd.

Though there are various forms of racism around the world, the most prominent is where white people belittle black people. Again, there is no apparent reason for this hate, but we may infer the *source* of this hate from America's history. Note that what is to follow is an immensely abbreviated version of the whole story—you should do your own research and study racism in America yourself.

Between the early-1600s and the mid-1800s, black people were captured from Africa and brought to the United States as slaves. When Britain first sailed to Africa in the late-1500s, they realized their technology and weaponry were unequivocally more advanced than Africa's. Hence, they started invading African territories and plundering their wealth. After Britain drained out Africa's wealth, they started enslaving the inhabitants. While the first slaves were taken to Europe, many more were transported to America. For over *250 years*, African slaves were put to agricultural labor in the United States, such as the cultivation of tobacco and cotton. In particular, following the invention of the cotton gin in 1793 (which significantly accelerated clothes manufacture), the United States called for the mass cultivation of cotton; countless African slaves were placed on cotton farms. Hence is why African slavery in America is often depicted by black people "picking cotton" (which means harvesting cotton flowers). Historians estimate that six to seven million people were imported and enslaved during the 18th century alone. Black people were *owned* by white people; the slaves endured brutal violence and mistreatment. The abolishment of African slavery began with the election of Abraham Lincoln as the president of the United States. Lincoln had strict anti-slavery views, which he actualized through the Civil War. The southern parts of America were climatically more suited for agriculture—therefore, slavery was more abundant in the south. Meanwhile, by the mid-1800s, the northern states of America began to recognize how wrong it was to force Africans to labor. After almost two years of war, Lincoln issued the *Emancipation Proclamation* on January 1, 1863, which stated that "all slaves shall be free henceforth." Unfortunately, this wasn't enough to end slavery—slavery in the United States met its official demise in 1865 after the 13th Amendment ("neither slavery nor involuntary servitude … shall exist within the United States …") was adopted.

So, the slaves were free—did that solve the problem? No. What followed was extreme and blatant racism. For over a century after the African slaves seized freedom, black people were severely discriminated by white people. To list a few examples: black people were not allowed on the same bus (or part of the bus) as white people, they were not allowed in the same restaurant as white people, they were not allowed to have the same jobs as white people, and they were not allowed to vote. Hate groups against black people emerged left and right, and many innocent black people were killed for no good reason. *Six thousand and five hundred black people are estimated to have been lynched* (i.e., murdered outside lawful prosecution, often by mobs) between 1865 and 1950. The horrific cases of Emmett Till, Thomas Moss, Calvin McDowell, Will Stewart, Thomas Shipp, and Abram Smith reveal a fraction of the gruesome reality.

We witness this form of black-white racism in *Maniac Magee*. To list a few relevant events from the book: an old black man in the East End gets enraged at Maniac for being part of the Beale family; Mars Bar gets mistreated by the white boys (a.k.a. the "Cobras") at Piper's birthday party at the McNab house; Grayson questions if black people perform the same basic acts as white people (like brushing their teeth and eating meatloaf). Interestingly, what seems to make Maniac truly furious is not the hate itself but the attitudes of the two races involved—Maniac is appalled that neither race tries to understand the other. The fact that both races simply exert hate and refuse to work together is absolutely absurd. Many readers will feel the same as Maniac. Perhaps this was the book's opinion on racism.

The book also pokes fun at racism and how both races involved barely comprehend each other's genuine circumstances. The black-white racism places absolute inferiority on black people—their overall living conditions are assumed to be miserable compared to the white people's. However, *Maniac Magee* claims that the exact opposite could equally be true. In the book, the Beales—a black family—has excellent living conditions: a clean house, caring parents, and proper education for the children. On the other hand, the McNabs—a white family—has objectively worse living conditions: a disgusting house, an irresponsible dad, and out-of-school children. As such, the racist white people, who often hold themselves up so much higher than black people, could, in reality, be the ones much lower.

With the memories of slavery becoming steadfastly hazy as time passes, racism against black people seems to be growing weaker and weaker. Nevertheless, there are still hints of racism left not only across the United States but also all over the world. For instance, the evidently intentional murder of George Floyd, a 46-year-old black man, by a white police officer in Minneapolis in 2020 enraged millions of people across America and drove them to partake in enormous protests amidst the COVID-19 pandemic.

Here's the takeaway on racism: it's *stupid*—hatred and discrimination without any reason should be strictly prohibited. But at the same time, we should realize that racism *is still present* and that *you can become the target too*, no matter which race you may be.

While this entire book is dedicated to the case of racism, there are some other concepts dissolved inside. One of the most prominent themes outside racism is the idea of *family and belonging*. Ever since Maniac lost his parents to the tragic trolly accident, he has been desperately looking for a home. At the start of the book, we see that Maniac is under the custody of his aunt and uncle, but he never realizes this place is his home. After he arrives in Two Mills, Maniac experiences a variety of families and caretakers—the Beale family, Grayson, and the McNab family—and learns that there are many dynamics to homes. To start, the Beale family is excellent: Mr. and Mrs. Beale take excellent care of their house and their children (as well as Maniac), and therefore all their children are well-behaved and mannered. There, Maniac feels loved and cared for and that he belongs. A direct contrast to the Beale family is the McNab family: the parents have divorced, and the alcoholic father never provides for his children; the children are extremely misbehaved, and the house is in utter chaos. Let alone not fitting in, Maniac didn't even want to be associated with the family (especially after Piper's disastrous birthday party). Grayson presents a unique case: he eventually grew close to Maniac, but he was far from proficient at looking after anyone other than himself. Grayson has lived many years alone, neither having to care for somebody nor being cared for by somebody else. Hence, he had forgotten how to nurture and love another person. Grayson was a great guardian to Maniac but never a good parent figure; he provided Maniac services only adults can offer—like buying him food and finding him a place to sleep—but he never became a father. At the end of the story, as expected, Maniac chooses the Beale family as his final destination. What do you think this book is trying to say about family? Does everyone have to be related to each other? Does everyone have to have the same skin color? Does everyone have to live together all the time? What truly matters in a family relationship?

Questions

1 Summary and First Impressions

A. Can you describe your favorite part of the story? Why do you like the part the most?

B. What do you think about the story? Do you like it?

2 Discussion Questions

A. Why do you think Two Mills is separated into two parts? Do you think the town has always been divided so? Could there have been a critical event that led to the separation?

B. Why do you think the whites and the blacks of Two Mills hate each other?

C. Maniac believes that if all the whites met Mrs. Beale and all the blacks met Mrs. Pickwell, their thoughts about each other will surely change. Do you agree with Maniac? Do you think such encounters will have an impact?

> **Reminder**
>
> Mrs. Beale is the kindhearted black lady who takes Manic in after realizing he doesn't have a home. Not only Mrs. Beale but the entire Beale family has no prejudice against white people—they consider racism ridiculous. Mrs. Pickwell is the charitable white lady who provides free meals to everyone struggling. Notably, she didn't even bat an eye when Maniac took Mars Bar—a black boy—to her house in the West End. While most white people there were startled by Mars Bar's presence, Mrs. Pickwell not only didn't care but also told her children to not make a fuss about Mars Bar's attendance.

D. Why do you think Mrs. Beale took Maniac in even though he was white?

E. Near the end of the book, Mars Bar rescues Russell, who was trapped atop the trolley bridge that spans the river. Do you think kind acts like this can help resolve the conflict between the two races in real life?

F. Father McNab is a complete abomination—he doesn't care about his household nor his children. He is always drinking and the McNab house is in utter chaos. However, is it still better to have a parent like him than not having one at all?

G. Why do you think Maniac wanted to help and look after Russell and Piper so much? Do you think he saw himself in the kids (in a way)?

H. Why do you think Maniac ran away from his aunt and uncle's house in the first place? What do you think he was looking for?

   i. Do you think Maniac truly found what he was looking for at the Beale house (at the end of the book)? Do you think he's going to stay put at the house this time and not run anymore?

I. How do you think the whites consider the blacks? Why does the McNabs think that the blacks will eventually cause an uprising?

J. How do you think the blacks consider the whites? Do you think they agree that the whites are better than them?

K. Had the story continued for longer, do you think the blacks and the whites of Two Mills could have eventually mixed-in and lived in harmony?

   i. Do you think Mars Bar saving Russell and Maniac living in the Beale house will influence the townspeople's thoughts?

L. Why do you think someone used Amanda's favorite book as confetti while celebrating Maniac solving the Cobble's Knot? Were they trying to mock the Beale family?

M. Excluding Maniac, think of the white characters in the book (the McNabs, Grayson, etc.), and think of the black characters in the book (the Beales, Mars Bar, etc.). Which side has more problems? Which side has more miserable lives? Do you think there's a reason why the author established the characters like this?

N. Have you ever witnessed (or heard of) racist practices around you? Can you explain the incident(s)?

Vocabulary Exercise

Instructions

These are some words and phrases used in *Maniac Magee*. Write each of their definition in English. Then, write a paragraph with the topic of your liking using <u>at least seven</u> of these words/phrases. Be mindful that one word/phrase can have multiple meanings or be used in more than one way. Carefully consider how the words and phrases were used in the original book, and try to use each word/phrase the same way as how the book used it.

Words & Phrases

commotion	practically	solitude	vacant	witness (*n.* or *v.*)
illusion	nonchalant	familiar	sneer	in an instant

Sentences from the book

Here are the sentences from the original book that contains the given words and phrases. Only use these as reference and do not write the same sentences for your exercise.

commotion: Laster on that first day, there was a **commotion** in the West End.

practically: "… 'mom, there's a boy I loaned one of my books out to!' 'Loaned a *book*? *You*?' Mom, he **practically** *made* me. He really likes books. I met him on–' …"

solitude: He loved the early morning. The "before-the-working-people time," he called it … He loved the silence and **solitude**.

vacant: He loved joining all the colors at the **vacant** lot and playing the summer days away.

witness (*n.* or *v.*): The **witnesses**—there were twice fifteen this time—went with him as far as Hector Street

illusion: It may have been an **illusion**, but it seemed that the hungrier he got, the farther Mrs. Pickwell's whistle traveled.

nonchalant: (Father) McNab smashed the tabletop; three fries and a bird wing jumped to the floor. "Now!" / John walked out, **nonchalantly** munching. "I was busy."

familiar: They were barely a block from Cobble's when Maniac heard a **familiar** voice.

sneer: "He ain't no cop. He's a *kid*." / "Yeah?" **sneered** Russel. "That's how much *you* know. They got cops that *look* like kids. That's how they catch kids."

in an instant: **In an instant**, he was bolt upright again, yanked by a hand he couldn't believe belonged to a girl.

Paragraph Write-up Exercise

Instructions

Write a short paragraph expressing your thoughts about the following questions. There are multiple questions to guide you arrange your thoughts and form your answer. Be sure to answer all the questions within a single paragraph—do not answer the questions individually.

A "paragraph" is a collection of sentences (which are not divided into separate lines) that convey a single idea throughout. The sentences in a paragraph must be logically arranged to coherently deliver your thoughts to the reader. A single paragraph must contain at least three sentences.

Question

How would the story have gone had Maniac been black? Which events from the book would change the most drastically? And how would Maniac turn out differently? What if all the characters' races were flipped?

Bibliography

1 – "racism" from *Encyclopedia Britannica* (https://www.britannica.com/topic/racism)

2 – "Slavery in America" from *History.com* (https://www.history.com/topics/black-history/slavery)

3 – "2020: The year America confronted racism" from *CNN* (https://edition.cnn.com/interactive/2020/12/us/america-racism-2020/)

4 – "LYNCHINGS IN AMERICA" from *History.com* (https://www.history.com/emmett-till-lynchings-activism)

About the Author

Jerry Spinelli (81; born Feb 1, 1941) is an American author born in Pennsylvania, U.S. He reviews various motifs closely related to children and young adults, such as sibling issues, loneliness, family troubles, conformity, etc. in his literature. His most well-known works include *Maniac Magee*, *Wringer*, *Stargirl*, and *Space Station Seventh Grade*.

http://jerryspinelliauthor.com/

Other Books by the Author

Columns of each table: (from left) Title of Book; Year Published; ATOS Book Level; Lexile Measure; Interest Level.

Guide to Interest Level:

LG (Lower Grades; suitable for grades K-3)

MG (Middle Grades; suitable for grades 4-8)

MG+ (Middle Grades Plus; suitable for grades 6+)

UG (Upper Grades; suitable for grades 9-12)

Stargirl Series				
Stargirl	2000	4.2	590L	UG
Love, Stargirl	2007	3.8	610L	UG

School Daze Series				
Report to the Principal's Office	1991	4.5	700L	MG
Who Ran My Underwear Up the Flagpole?	1992	5.0	740L	MG
Do the Funky Pickle	1992	4.0	670L	MG
Picklemania	1993	4.3	610L	MG

Novels				
Maniac Magee *1991 Newbery Medal	1990	4.7	820L	MG
Crash	1996	3.6	HL560L	MG
The Library Card	1997	4.3	690L	MG
Wringer *1998 Newbery Honor	1997	4.5	690L	MG
Loser	2002	4.3	710L	MG
Milkweed	2003	3.6	510L	MG
Eggs	2007	3.6	540L	MG
Smiles to Go	2008	3.3	HL490L	MG+
Jake and Lily	2012	3.2	480L	MG
Hokey Pokey	2013	3.6	HL600L	MG+
Dead Wednesday	2021	3.9	HL550L	MG

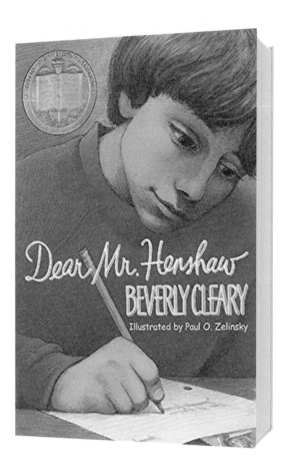

Dear Mr. Henshaw

by Beverly Cleary

Published	1983 (1984 Newbery Medal)
ATOS Book Level	4.9
Lexile	910L
Word Count	18145

Talk about a book with a fascinating style! *Dear Mr. Henshaw* is a compilation of letters and diary entries written by Leigh Botts, a sixth-grader (for most of the book) struggling with family troubles. Leigh's favorite author is Mr. Boyd Henshaw; he has written fan letters to him since second grade. Sadly, Leigh doesn't get a response until sixth grade: Leigh contacts Mr. Henshaw concerning his assignment, 'Write a letter to your favorite author and ask them ten questions,' for which he receives a half-hearted, joking reply from Mr. Henshaw, along with ten additional questions for *him* to answer in return. Albeit annoyed by the extra work, Leigh decides to accept this challenge—partly because his mother forced him to but also because he loves to write. Leigh dreams of becoming as successful an author as Mr. Henshaw; unfortunately, his family issue is distracting him from working toward this dream. Leigh lives with only his mom, as his parents got divorced not too long ago. It turns out his father is a trucker who prefers life on the road over being a father. At first, Leigh resents his father for abandoning his family, but the more he writes about him, the more he starts to understand his old man and comes to terms with his current situation. In the meantime, his writing skills mature as quickly as his thoughts, evidently witnessed in his pieces. Near the end, Leigh finally gets to confront his father as he visits home during his delivery. Despite his extended absence and hence the awkward atmosphere, Leigh's father conjures up the courage to ask Leigh's mother for reunition. What will her answer be, and what shall happen to Leigh's family?

Themes

Yet another Newbery-awarded book about family troubles, this one. But there's a twist to this book: it combines the (somewhat) trite topic with the concept of *writing*. The book insinuates how *writing* can be an excellent outlet for confessing one's true thoughts and emotions. In the book, Leigh gradually begins to cope with his situation by writing about his life and decompressing his mind. Likewise, it's sometimes powerful and potentially essential to write down what's going on inside your head on a piece of paper. We must acknowledge and accept that even we ourselves often do not comprehend our minds entirely. That's why we need to have conversations with ourselves. Some may be able to do so inside their heads, but it's more intuitive to write it out. We can only start improving ourselves by learning who we truly are and how we truly feel.

Related to the above, it's also easy to overlook the power of *handwriting*. Writing on paper with a pen or a pencil engenders a totally different set of emotions than typing on a keyboard. Your train of thought flows more naturally and candidly when you write with your hand; it allows you to be true to yourself. In addition, you can refer back to your mistakes when writing with your hand. Whenever you note something you're dissatisfied with, you can move on to the next page instead of erasing what you've written. While deleting your writing on the PC is as easy as holding down "Backspace," it's not so convenient when you use a pen or a pencil. Ironically, it helps to retain all your attempts—even the ones you deemed mediocre initially. What you didn't like the first time could become your preferred later. Generally, keeping rough drafts and previous attempts is rarer when typing. On a different note, someone's handwriting can give so much information about them. The size of the letters, legibility, alignment, etc., can grant you a surprisingly deep understanding of one's true emotions and thoughts.

Here's a fun activity for you: try following through Leigh's writing while paying attention to *how his writing skills advance*. Conspicuous advances occur to his spelling and grammar (which were in absolute chaos back in second grade). But not only that, subtle enhancements continue to take place in Leigh's writing throughout the book. First, it gets more descriptive— he uses adjectives and adverbs more frequently and effectively to enrich his sentences. Furthermore, his vocabulary grows more and more sophisticated. Finally, he starts producing longer, grammatically complex sentences with multiple phrases and clauses. If you're not grammar-savvy yet, you may have missed some of these changes. However, if you look close enough, you'll notice a lot of improvements in his writing.

And, of course, this book contains several aspects of *family trouble*—especially those related to *the parents' divorce*. Divorce is a hard pill to swallow for the married and even more for their children. Nonetheless, it will be the correct decision if the family is suffering. Divorce is neither weird nor uncommon. While the married couple must always take responsibility for their relationship and dedicate all their efforts to maintain it, when the relationship reaches an irreparable state, divorce may be a wise choice. Unfortunately, it doesn't mean that the pain lessens; the event could be traumatic to both the parents and their children. Throughout the book, we see how Leigh struggles with his father's absence—he gets frustrated every time his dad forgets to call him and is deeply shocked when he realizes he might be moving on to another woman and another kid.

Yet the book also presents a brighter opposite to this family saga: amid the void of paternal care, Leigh finds comfort in other male adults nearby—namely, Mr. Henshaw and Mr. Fridley.

Understanding Leigh's situation and feeling pitiful, they both act as father/grandfather figures for Leigh—they listen to his concerns, give him advice on his life and career, and congratulate him on his achievements. Hence, although Leigh doesn't have his biological father with him, he feels protected and secure under the supervision of these two men. This happens in real life too: albeit seldom, children who don't have a parent (or both parents) tend to locate a "father figure" and/or a "mother figure" from adult males and females around them. As a child, it's natural that you desire (and require) an adult to lean on, and good adults will gladly open their arms and accept the guardian position. However, remember that there aren't only good adults out there, unfortunately.

Questions

① Summary and First Impressions

A. Can you describe your favorite part of the story? Why do you like the part the most?

B. What do you think about the story? Do you like it?

② Discussion Questions

A. As you would have noticed, this book displays a fascinating style of writing. What do you think about the way this book is written?

> **Chew on this**
>
> The entire text of *Dear Mr. Henshaw* is a collection of the letters Leigh writes to Mr. Henshaw, plus Leigh's diary entries. Some of the previous books also experiment with various styles of writing—for example, *Al Capone Does My Shirts* was in the form of the main character Moose's diary, and *From the Mixed-up Files of Mrs. Basil E. Frankweiler* was in the form of a letter from Mrs. Frankweiler to her lawyer, Saxonberg. Nevertheless, no other book capitalizes on incorporating unique writing styles as impactfully as *Dear Mr. Henshaw*. While most books eventually conform to the conventional third-person narrative fashion of storytelling, *Dear Mr. Henshaw* goes "all-in" with the letters and diary style. This makes the book all the more unique and attractive.

B. We can tell that Mr. Henshaw replies occasionally to Leigh's letters (Leigh mentions Mr. Henshaw's advices in a few of his letters). However, the book never discloses Mr. Henshaw's letters. We may only guess what he said from Leigh's letters. Is it more interesting that you cannot read Mr. Henshaw's letters? Or is it more annoying? Do you think it would have been better if they had been included in the book, or do you like it the way it is?

C. Did you notice that Leigh's writing skills constantly improve throughout the book? What about his writing changes?

D. Leigh's father is not at home, and this is one of the plot points that drives the story. Due to his absence, does Leigh find some "father figures" near him? Who do you think are these father figures?

    i.   Is Mr. Henshaw one?

    ii.   Is Mr. Fridley one?

E. How does Leigh's thoughts about his father change throughout the story (especially near the end)? Why do they change that way?

F. Do you agree with Mr. Henshaw's advices on writing? What's the best advice that he gives to Leigh, in your opinion?

G. Do you think writing helps Leigh cope with the issues in his life (especially his family issues)? How, and why does writing help him?

    i.   Do you think writing about yourself (and your current situation) can be an effective outlet for your confusion and/or negative emotions?

H. Why do you think Leigh's mom refused to reunite with her ex-husband at the end of the story?

I. Have you ever written a fan mail to anyone? Did you ever get a response?

    i.   If you were to write a fan letter now, who would it be to?

Vocabulary Exercise

Instructions

These are some words and phrases used in *Dear Mr. Henshaw*. Write each of their definition in English. Then, write a paragraph with the topic of your liking using at least seven of these words/phrases. Be mindful that one word/phrase can have multiple meanings or be used in more than one way. Carefully consider how the words and phrases were used in the original book, and try to use each word/phrase the same way as how the book used it.

Words & Phrases

satisfied (*adj.*)	urgent	excuse (*n.*)	nuisance	grateful
demonstration	blame	ordinary	examine	experience

Sentences from the book

Here are the sentences from the original book that contains the given words and phrases. Only use these as reference and do not write the same sentences for your exercise.

satisfied (*adj.*): I hope you are **satisfied** for making me do all this extra work.

urgent: I need your answer by next Friday. This is **urgent**!

excuse (*n.*): Mom says not to worry about the postage, so I can't use that as an excuse for not answering.

nuisance: I don't think I can keep a diary. I don't want to be a **nuisance** to you, but I wish you could tell me how. I am stuck.

grateful: Thanks for the tip. I know you're busy. / Your **grateful** friend, / Leigh Botts

demonstration: I let her in and gave her a **demonstration** of my burglar alarm.

blame: I felt a little better when Mom said she was tired of life on the road. Maybe I wasn't to **blame** after all.

ordinary: I found an **ordinary** light switch, a little battery and a cheat doorbell.

examine: The principal, who always prowls around keeping an eye on things at lunchtime, came over to **examine** my lunchbox.

experience: I tried to start a story called *The Great Lunchbox Mystery*, but I couldn't seem to turn my lunchbox **experience** into a story because I didn't know who the thief (thieves) was (were), and I don't want to know.

Paragraph Write-up Exercise

Instructions

Write a short paragraph expressing your thoughts about the following questions. There are multiple questions to guide you arrange your thoughts and form your answer. Be sure to answer all the questions within a single paragraph—do not answer the questions individually.

A "paragraph" is a collection of sentences (which are not divided into separate lines) that convey a single idea throughout. The sentences in a paragraph must be logically arranged to coherently deliver your thoughts to the reader. A single paragraph must contain at least three sentences.

Question

Write a fan mail to the author of your favorite book in the book club. Explain about your favorite character and your favorite event from the book. Remember to keep the proper format of a letter and be polite and sincere to the author.

Bibliography

About the Author

Beverly Atlee Cleary (born Apr 12, 1916; died Mar 25, 2021, aged 104) was an American children and young-adults' author born in Oregon, U.S. She was one of the most successful American authors in history. She was expert at portraying the lives of children growing up in middle-class families with incredible realism. She proficiently highlighted the virtues of life which may be minute to adults yet sizable to children. Her characters received a lot of sympathy from her readers, who could understand and resonate with the situations and the feelings her characters were experiencing. Her most well-known works include *Dear Mr. Henshaw*, *The Mouse and the Motorcycle*, the *Ramona* series, and the *Henry Huggins* series.

https://www.beverlycleary.com/

Other Books by the Author

Columns of each table: (from left) Title of Book; Year Published; ATOS Book Level; Lexile Measure; Interest Level.

Guide to Interest Level:

LG (Lower Grades; suitable for grades K-3)

MG (Middle Grades; suitable for grades 4-8)

MG+ (Middle Grades Plus; suitable for grades 6+)

UG (Upper Grades; suitable for grades 9-12)

Leigh Botts Series				
Dear Mr. Henshaw *1984 Newbery Medal	1983	4.9	910L	MG
Strider	1994	4.8	840L	MG

Ralph S. Mouse Series				
The Mouse and the Motor Cycle	1965	5.1	860L	MG
Runaway Ralph	1970	5.3	890L	MG
Ralph S. Mouse	1982	5.1	860L	MG

Ramona Quimby Series				
Beezus and Ramona	1955	4.8	780L	MG
Ramona the Pest	1968	5.1	850L	MG
Ramona the Brave	1975	4.9	820L	MG
Ramona and Her Father *1978 Newbery Honor	1977	5.2	840L	MG
Ramona and Her Mother	1979	4.8	860L	MG
Ramona Quimby, Age 8 *1982 Newbery Honor	1981	5.6	860L	MG
Ramona Forever	1984	4.8	810L	MG
Ramona's World	1999	4.8	750L	MG

Henry Huggins Series				
Henry Huggins	1950	4.7	670L	MG
Henry and Beezus	1952	4.6	730L	MG
Henry and Ribsy	1954	4.6	740L	MG
Henry and the Paper Route	1957	5.3	820L	MG
Henry and the Clubhouse	1962	5.1	820L	MG
Ribsy	1964	5.0	820L	MG

Ellen & Otis Series				
Ellen Tebbits	1951	4.9	740L	MG
Otis Spofford	1953	4.6	720L	MG

First Love Series				
Fifteen	1956	5.4	870L	UG
The Luckiest Girl	1975	5.9	910L	MG
Jean and Johnny	1959	5.6	900L	MG
Sister of the Bride	1963	5.9	880L	MG

Novels				
Emily's Runaway Imagination	1961	6.1	910L	MG
Mitch and Amy	1967	6.2	950L	MG
Socks	1973	5.2	890L	MG
Muggie Maggie	1990	4.5	730L	IG

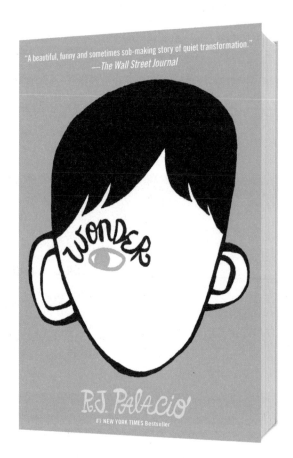

"A beautiful, funny and sometimes sob-making story of quiet transformation."
—*The Wall Street Journal*

WONDER

R.J. PALACIO

#1 NEW YORK TIMES Bestseller

Wonder

by R. J. Palacio

Published	2012 (2013 Carnegie Medal)
ATOS Book Level	4.8
Lexile	790L
Word Count	73053

ave you ever heard of the "seven wonders of the world"? Well, make that *eight* because we've got another one coming: August "Auggie" Pullman. Auggie bears a rare genetic disorder that curses him with a list of impairments, including tiny ears, misplaced eyes, and a cleft palate. His looks are enough to make a small child cry (which has actually happened several times before), and poor Auggie is well aware of this. There was even a time when he refused to go outside without his astronaut helmet on to hide his face—though he doesn't wear it anymore, he's still unhappy with his looks. Fortunately, Auggie has been homeschooled his entire life—*until now*. With Auggie turning twelve, his parents decide that it's about time for him to attend school. The first weeks pass exactly how Auggie expected: the school kids sneak peek at him, talk behind his back, and deliberately avoid him. Thankfully, not *everyone* is like that: Jack, the widely well-received, and Summer, the open-minded, lend their shoulders for Auggie to lean on. Unfortunately, Julian, the most popular kid in fifth grade, blatantly displays disgust regarding Auggie's looks, and many follow suit. However, everybody grows up—gradually, the school kids start seeing past Auggie's looks. Soon, they realize that, in truth, Auggie is just the same as them—if not *better*. They recognize how caring, supportive, and humorous Auggie can be. (Not to mention how smart he is.) After the winter break, Auggie emerges as the fifth-grade superstar; by the end of the school year, everyone (except Julian) becomes his ally. (Even Julian's three henchmen, Miles, Amos, and Henry, help Auggie escape from seventh-grader bullies.) Bearing such attractiveness that overcompensates his unfortunate appearance, Auggie is definitely worthy of the title: *wonder*.

Themes

Don't judge a book by its cover—this proverb probably summarizes Auggie's tale the best. The school could be unforgiving to those who are different. Teenagers often desperately try to be "cool" by conforming to a single "trend"; to stand out from the crowd generally means isolation or bullying. Having even the most trivial quirks is enough to turn you into the target—imagine if you had a face as conspicuous as Auggie's. Perhaps Auggie was destined for negative attention from the very beginning. Nevertheless, middle school is where the magic starts kicking in, and a crucial part of the magic is *coming of age*. As kids begin to mature, they realize how hollow it is to set someone's appearance as the "butt of the joke"—they recognize what matters is what's *inside*. The more the kids awaken, the more they start liking Auggie—for under his possibly disturbing face lies a sincere, entertaining, and intelligent mind.

Seeing past someone's appearance is not the only aspect of growing up the book handles. For the older audience, Via's tale may also pierce deep into their hearts. Olivia "Via" Pullman, Auggie's older sister, experiences a major *identity crisis* as she enters high school. Having always been the protective, loving older sister, Via breaks apart as she grasps that she no longer wants to be defined by her beloved brother. Before, Via was proud of the title: "the older sister of August Pullman, the kid with a peculiar face." But now, she wants to be known as herself, "Olivia Pullman." As she enters a faraway high school, she hides her childhood nickname "Via" and introduces herself as "Olivia"; she also avoids mentioning Auggie to any of her new friends. While she is pleased to finally claim the center of her life (which used to be Auggie before), she also feels guilty that she may no longer be the excellent older sister she was glad to be. It is natural (and obligatory) to want to discover your true identity as you grow up. The most critical elements of maturity include: learning what you want to accomplish, what you want to be known for, and what kind of life you aspire to achieve. Unfortunately, Via's circumstances are against her favor because of her special-needs brother. Thankfully, she holds herself together with the support of her boyfriend, Justin, and her loving parents.

Wonder also captures *teenage angst* quite effectively. Everybody goes through the phase of craving attention and striving to become the "cool kid." During such time, everybody also admires the "cool kids" and wishes to be part of the "cool kids' group." Many elements can define a "cool kid"—knowing and practicing the "trends," being fashionable, athleticism, and—in some twisted way—bullying and overpowering weaker kids. In the book, the leading "cool kid" is Julian; consequently, many conform to his opinions and behaviors. In its early stages, kids did not hang out with Auggie or even go close to him (following Julian's disapproval toward Auggie). That's why Summer's simple act of 'sitting next to Auggie during lunch' was so incredibly gossiped over and why Jack badmouthed Auggie on Halloween, although he didn't mean any of his words. (As you can see, even as nice of a kid as Jack also goes through teenage angst.) Nevertheless, as the kids grow up, most eventually realize how meaningless this "you're cool, you're not cool" act is. Unfortunately, it seems like Julian still hasn't learned his lesson by the end of the book—maybe one day.

Coming out of your comfort zone: Auggie does a lot of that in the book. When he was younger, he had his astronaut helmet to "protect" him, but he is forced to take it off. And going to school is an enormous challenge for him. At first, it hurts him—he struggles to pull himself out of bed in the morning and suffers from the 'whispering behind his backs' and weird looks. Yet, eventually, he starts enjoying school, and everyone else starts enjoying his company. I admit: it's unmistakably comfy to roll yourself up into a blanket burrito and lay on your bed all day, but sometimes, you've *got* to pop that bubble. Get out there, accept challenges, and face defeat—not only will you grow a thick skin, but you'll also end up enjoying the whole ride.

Here are a few other bite-sized topics. First, each family in the book has one problem or the other—Miranda's parents are divorced, Justin's parents never gave him enough love, Summer's father was killed in action, Jack's family is financially struggling, and Julian's family is overly sensitive. Practically the only family that's "normal" is Auggie's. While he may not have been blessed with his appearance, he has certainly been blessed with a fantastic family—which is *as*, if not *more*, important than having good looks. The book also presents the discussion between *kindness* and *niceness*. During Auggie's first school tour, Charlotte is *nice* to Auggie. Comparatively, making the initial approach (sitting next to Auggie during lunch) and continuing to reach out to Auggie, Summer is *kind*. Can you spot the difference?

Although remote from the concept of "themes," it's worthwhile to mention that *Wonder* is *packed* with easter eggs. First, the book contains several real-life references (i.e., homages) that reflect children's genuine interests. (Well, perhaps they're a bit outdated, considering the book came out in 2012.) For example, Auggie is a big fan of the *Star Wars* franchise; Jack mentions Auggie owns an Xbox 360 and plays *Halo* (when he goes over to Auggie's house for their science fair project); Jack messages Auggie through Facebook (after he punches Julian in the face). Within Jack and Auggie's texts, we find another fun easter egg: the book effectively reflects teenagers' language and slang (which may also be outdated now). In their texts, we witness words like "frenz (= friends)," "awsum = (awesome)," and "urself (= yourself)" which are some grammar-breaking shorthand notions teens (may) use in their texts. Finally, the book also uses several great songs as innuendos. For example, one of *Part One's* chapters is named: "Wake Me Up When September Ends," which is the title of a wonderful song by Green Day, and the nickname Miranda gave to Auggie, "Major Tom," is a reference to yet another fantastic song: "Space Oddity" by David Bowie. As you can see, the book contains so many easter eggs to be discovered. *The more you know!*

Lastly, we must discuss the brilliant writing style of this book. When we consider a single part of the book in isolation, we can identify that it is in the first-person narrative. This style offers the unchallenged asset that the reader can thoroughly comprehend the main character's thoughts and emotions. However, its critical drawback is that the other characters' thoughts are barely revealed. In a first-person narrated book, the main character's eyes are our windows to the plot—just as how we are unsure what's going through someone's head in reality, the main character has little idea what the other characters are thinking. In *Wonder*, however, the author ingeniously tackles this issue by *introducing various perspectives*. The book features eight parts, written from six different characters' points of view; a single event is mentioned multiple times from the perspective of everyone involved. By doing so, every character's thoughts and emotions become completely uncovered in the end. It's also fascinating to collect the scattered pieces of each event one by one to finish the puzzle and reveal all of its secrets.

Questions

(1) **Summary and First Impressions**

    A. Can you describe your favorite part of the story? Why do you like the part the most?

    B. What do you think about the story? Do you like it?

(2) **Discussion Questions**

    A. Why do you think Jack badmouthed Auggie on Halloween day? Why did he want to hide to Julian that he likes Auggie?

> **Reminder**
>
> Auggie had to switch his costume urgently on the morning of Halloween day. Therefore, no one noticed him when he went to school (in a different costume). When he arrived at his classroom, he saw Jack talking with Julian and some other boys. Not realizing that Auggie entered the classroom, Jack insults Auggie, saying he would kill himself if he were him. Auggie, deeply shocked by his best friend's betrayal, leaves the classroom to cry in a bathroom stall. Jack and Auggie's friendship breaks apart momentarily following this event.

    B. Why do you think Miranda avoided Via during most of the semester? Why did Miranda feel bad about lying Auggie is her brother?

        i.   Why did Miranda tell such a lie? How did she try to justify herself?

    C. Why do you think Julian's mother got so aggravated about Auggie being in the same school as her son? Do you think she's on the right page?

D. Why do you think "The Plague" died down after the winter break? Why were the kids no longer actively avoiding Auggie? Why were they treating him nicely? Was there a decisive event?

> **Reminder**
>
> "The Plague" was a game created by Julian that was, in truth, blatant bullying of Auggie. The rules of this "game" were that no one was to touch Auggie, and had one come in contact with him, they would have to wash their hands immediately, or they shall share the same fate. While most schoolkids participated in The Plague early into the school year, practically no one continued it after the winter break. On the contrary, everyone started being friendly to Auggie and hanging out with him more.

E. Why do you think Via hid the fact that Auggie was her brother to her new friends at high school?

    i.   Why do you think Via was hesitant to invite her own parents to the school show? Did Auggie have a hand in this?

F. Why do you think Miranda faked being sick to give Via a chance at the school play?

> **Reminder**
>
> Both Miranda and Via applied for the lead heroine of the school play. Miranda triumphed and got the part, while Via was accepted as the understudy. On the opening night, Miranda noticed that both Via's parents and Auggie came (while no one related to her came), and she decided to fake being ill to yield Via the opportunity to perform.

    i.   Do you think she would have done the same thing even if her mother and/or her boyfriend were/was present at the opening night?

G. How do you think staying away from home for four weeks (at her grandparents' house) affect Via on how she perceives Auggie? Do you think her attitude toward Auggie would have been different had she never been away from home?

> **Reminder**
>
> When Via was younger, she had stayed away from Auggie (and her parents) for four weeks at her grandparents' house. She describes when she returned home and reunited with Auggie, for a short moment, she saw Auggie as perhaps how other people see him. While she explains that her perception returned to normal soon, she suspects the event may have permanently affected how she treats Auggie.

H. How do you think having Auggie as a little brother influenced Via's personalities? Would she have been markedly different had she never had a special brother like Auggie?

I. Do you think the story would have been different if Jack and Auggie hadn't become friends in the beginning? Does Jack's reputation/popularity at school help Auggie adjust?

J. Did you notice that Justin's section has broken grammar? The section is missing critical punctuations and capitalizations. Why do you think this is the case?

Chew on this

I (the author) played trombone for seven years through middle school and high school. And I remember thinking back then, especially when I would get into the really low notes, that notes on a musical staff looked like lowercase letters of the alphabet ... So, when it came to writing from Justin's point of view, because he's a musician, ... it seemed natural for me to use lowercase letters to represent his thoughts in a very visual way. He's the kind of person who doesn't talk a lot, because he's naturally shy, but has a lot going on inside. The running monologue inside his head has no time for capital letters or punctuation ... - R. J. Palacio (the author), wonderthebook.com/about > FAQ's)

K. Why do you think Auggie's parents wanted to send him to school? What do you think they were anticipating? Do you think there's a bigger reason than his education?

L. How is the Pullman family different from all the other families introduced in the story?

Hint

Consider if the other families have any problems or missing persons. Including the Pullman (i.e., Auggie's) family, there were seven families mentioned in the book: Auggie's family, Summer's family, Jack's family, Miranda's family, Justin's family, and Julian's family.

M. Why do you think Auggie's father threw away his astronaut helmet? Why do you think his father thought it would help his son more?

N. How does Auggie's attitude toward his own appearance change throughout the story?

Vocabulary Exercise

Instructions

These are some words and phrases used in *Wonder*. Write each of their definition in English. Then, write a paragraph with the topic of your liking using <u>at least seven</u> of these words/phrases. Be mindful that one word/phrase can have multiple meanings or be used in more than one way. Carefully consider how the words and phrases were used in the original book, and try to use each word/phrase the same way as how the book used it.

Words & Phrases

| motivate | interrupt | severe | catastrophe | stay on top of |
| majority | outrageous | remote | hysterically | accommodate |

Sentences from the book

Here are the sentences from the original book that contains the given words and phrases. Only use these as reference and do not write the same sentences for your exercise.

motivate: "... Like a famous quote. Like a line from a fortune cookie. Any saying or ground rule that can **motivate** you."

interrupt: "I don't want them to come to the show, Justin," she **interrupts** impatiently.

severe: He has a **severe** overbite and an extremely undersized jawbone.

catastrophe: Does August see himself as he might have looked without that single gene that caused the **catastrophe** of his face?

stay on top of: I've gotten used to figuring things out on my own: ... how to **stay on top of** my schoolwork so I never fall behind in class.

majority: It was starting to feel like the **majority** of the boys weren't buying into Julian anymore.

outrageous: Davenport looked furious. "Miranda, this is **outrageous**."

remote: So on opening night no one that was **remotely** close to me was even there.

hysterically: Via nodded, but she was crying **hysterically** now.

accommodate: They (eyes) bulge outward because his eye cavities are too shallow to **accommodate** them.

Paragraph Write-up Exercise

Instructions

Write a short paragraph expressing your thoughts about the following questions. There are multiple questions to guide you arrange your thoughts and form your answer. Be sure to answer all the questions within a single paragraph—do not answer the questions individually.

A "paragraph" is a collection of sentences (which are not divided into separate lines) that convey a single idea throughout. The sentences in a paragraph must be logically arranged to coherently deliver your thoughts to the reader. A single paragraph must contain at least three sentences.

Question

Write a short chapter for the book based on a perspective of a character that was <u>not</u> included in the book. In the book, the perspectives of August, Via, Summer, Jack, Justin, and Miranda were shown.

Bibliography

1 – "ABOUT THE AUTHOR" from *Wonder by R.J. Palacio*
(https://wonderthebook.com/about)

About the Author

Raquel Jaramillo Palacio (59; born Jul 13, 1964) is an American author and graphic designer born in New York, U.S. She was more active as an illustrator early in her career, and she designed countless book covers and children's books (including her own). *Wonder* was her debut novel, yet it ended up becoming a homerun. She is most well-known for *Wonder* and its sequels, which includes: *Auggie & Me: Three Wonder Stories*, *365 Days of Wonder: Mr. Browne's Book of Precepts*, and *We're All Wonders*.

https://wonderthebook.com/books

Other Books by the Author

Columns of each table: (from left) Title of Book; Year Published; ATOS Book Level; Lexile Measure; Interest Level.

Guide to Interest Level:
LG (Lower Grades; suitable for grades K-3)
MG (Middle Grades; suitable for grades 4-8)
MG+ (Middle Grades Plus; suitable for grades 6+)
UG (Upper Grades; suitable for grades 9-12)

Novels				
Pony	2021	5.1	740L	MG

Wonder Series

Auggie and Me is the most notable sequel to the original book. It ties three stories: *The Julian Chapter*, *Pluto*, and *Shingaling* together. Each of the three presents an additional perspective (of a character) that was not made use in the original book. *The Julian Chapter* provides Julian's perspective on several of the original book's events; *Pluto* provides Christopher's (Auggie's oldest friend) perspective and sheds light on Auggie's earlier life before Beecher Prep; and *Shingaling* provides Charlotte's perspective and reveals the girls' intake on some of the original book's events. The three stories were initially published individually, but were combined later on under the heading *Auggie and Me*.

Wonder *2013 Carnegie Medal	2012	4.8	790	MG
365 Days of Wonder: Mr. Browne's PRECEPTS	2014		740L	MG
The Julian Chapter	2014	4.3	680L ↓	MG
Pluto	2015	4.2	680L ↓	MG
Shingaling	2015	4.7	680L ↓	MG
White Bird	2017	3.5	GN440L	MG

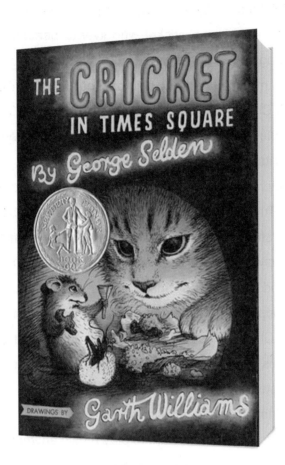

The Cricket in Times Square

by George Selden

Published	1960 (1961 Newbery Honor)
ATOS Book Level	4.9
Lexile	780L
Word Count	25278

Plot Introduction

Soothing yet powerful, balanced yet versatile—music is indeed *the spice of life*. Our hero today is Chester, a music-loving cricket who lives a peaceful life in Connecticut. His favorite activity is to lean against a tree stump and play music by rubbing his legs together. One day, Chester enters a mouth-watering picnic basket and gets trapped. The basket came all the way from New York City, and as the picnickers return home, Chester has no choice but to follow. After a long, painful train ride, Chester arrives at Times Square station. He is taken in by Mario (whose parents run a newsstand inside the station). Mario makes Chester a makeshift bed using a matchbox and convinces his parents to keep him. That night, Chester makes two more friends: Tucker, the rat, and Harry, the cat; they both reside in the station. After Chester settles in, he shares his musical talent with his new animal friends. Unfortunately, Tucker gets too carried away by Chester's music and accidentally knocks off the matchbox. A fire starts in the newsstand, and the newspapers and magazines get damaged. This ticks Mario's mom off—she disapproved of Chester from the beginning and is now absolutely ready to kick him out. Just then, Chester lets out a chirp of mama's favorite song, and this changes her thought. Touched by his music, mama forgives Chester and lets him stay. Not only that: Mario's parents allow Chester to perform in front of their customers. They all get captivated by his music; Chester gains fame, Mario's family earns money, and all seems to be going great. But, one day, Chester decides he doesn't want to play music anymore and wishes to return to Connecticut. What made him give up his favorite activity, and what will happen next?

Themes

Can you guess what the principal theme of this book is? *Music*—so cryptic, isn't it? Jokes aside, this book presents the perfect opportunity for us to consider *music*. Music is one of the very few things in this world that is universally appreciated—good music is praised by people from all cultures and backgrounds. Even if the lyrics are in a language you don't understand, you can still cherish the tune, melody, and rhythm. Music also has so many influences on humans. The most prominent is, perhaps, to *make us experience varied emotions*. With its construction—the melody, chord progression, rhythm, and tempo—and its lyrics combined, a song makes us go through a particular set of feelings. The songwriter, in turn, can convey those emotions by carefully arranging their song. Therein, we find another astonishing power of music—*communication*. Even if a song doesn't have lyrics, it can transmit complex emotions via its composition. And with lyrics, songs can send more specific, direct messages. As for some other capacities, music can trigger nostalgia, make us recall particular instances of memory, or help us concentrate or fall asleep. Now, think about music from *your* perspective—how do you consume music, and how does music affect you?

The book also questions *the concept of "home."* One's "home" is commonly defined as 'the place one lives permanently, usually as a part of a family'; it's where one ultimately returns to at the end of the day. Generally, you'd only refer to a *single* location as your "home," but is that always true—can a person only have *one* home at a given time? To take this further, how *should* we define one's "home"? Perhaps your "home" isn't necessarily where you come back to sleep every day. Maybe your home is where you have people who care for and love you. Even if you do not lie down and sleep inside the place, as long as you have people who provide comfort and security, it could be your "home." In the book, Chester leaves Connecticut, where he lived his entire life, and moves to New York City, a completely different place he's never been. Despite the unfamiliar surroundings, Chester soon *feels* home thanks to all the great friends he makes. Perhaps we cannot label Times Square station his new address— regardless, he feels content there. Relatedly, maybe the *group of people* present at the location is the most decisive factor when considering your "home." If so, you could have *multiple* homes—any place containing people of the aforementioned qualities would be your "home." Or, perhaps, the set of *emotions* you feel at the location is what matters the most. At your home, you feel secure, comfortable, and relaxed. A place that yields such positive emotions would be worthy of calling your "home." And just as before, this place need not be the same place you lay your head down every night. What do you say? How would you define your home? What is the most critical element for you when it comes to your "home"? And how many homes do you think you have right now?

The final noteworthy topic in the book is *your hobby vs. your job*. To never transform your hobby into your profession is common yet imperative advice. People often believe that the only reason they enjoy their hobby is that they appreciate the activity involved. However, the entertainment provided by your hobby often results from the *combination* of the activity and *freedom*. Your hobby is so charming because you only do it *occasionally*. If you did it every day or under a fixed schedule, it would surely become tedious. Unfortunately, this aspect of hobbies is often overlooked—you only realize the importance of freedom once you start working under a timetable. In the book, Chester's favorite activity is playing music. As a cricket, he could let out beautiful chirps by rubbing his legs together; this was his go to pastime back in Connecticut. Chester still enjoyed playing music after he moved to New York City until he started to perform for the newsstand visitors. But it's not the stage fright that gets him—it's the *consistent schedule*. Before, Chester played music whenever he wanted to, but now, he must play according to a program. Just like how we are not always in the mood to commit to our hobbies, Chester is not always in the mood to play. Nevertheless, the scheduled performances continue until he completely burns out and refuses to play anymore. Likewise, even your favorite activity can get old once you start doing it too frequently or under a set plan. It's best to leave hobbies as hobbies and separate your job from your hobby.

Questions

① Summary and First Impressions

A. Can you describe your favorite part of the story? Why do you like the part the most?

B. What do you think about the story? Do you like it?

② Discussion Questions

A. What would you do if you accidentally arrived somewhere far away from your home by getting on the wrong public transportation? Would you like to explore the place first or return home as fast as possible?

    i.   If you made friends at the faraway place, would that inspire you to stay there more, or would you like to go back home regardless? What about Chester? Do you think he would have stayed in New York City for long even if he had never met Mario, Harry, and Tucker?

    ii.   (For the younger audience:) Are you okay with using public transport on your own?

B. Throughout the book, many characters are taken away by Chester's music. Do you think music is powerful enough to move someone's heart? Have you ever had such an experience yourself?

    i.   Do you think music can be used to send a message? Can music without any lyrics still send a message? Can music be used as a means of communication?

C. What defines a "home"? How would you define your "home"? Between the location of your home and the people at your home, which side is more important to you?

i. If you're at your home by yourself, would it still feel like home?

ii. If you went on a vacation with your whole family, would the accommodation feel like home?

iii. If your family just moved to a new place, how long would it take before the new place starts feeling like home?

D. Recall the time when Chester accidentally ate half of a two-dollar bill. Tucker suggested many ideas to cover up the incident, but Chester rejected them all. Why do you think Chester didn't try to hide his mistake?

i. In the story, Chester was caught red-handed by Mama Bellini while he was contemplating what to do. Do you think Chester could have acted differently for a better outcome? Do you think it would have been better for him had he tried to hide his mistake? Or, do you think there was no other option?

E. Why do you think Chester got sick of playing music, even though it was his favorite activity?

i. Do you think even your favorite activity can get old if you repeat it enough times?

ii. Do you think even your favorite activity can get old if you perform it according to a fixed schedule?

iii. Would you be okay to perform your favorite activity in front of an audience?

F. Why do you think Chester decided to go back to Connecticut (toward the end of the story) even though he was now comfortable in New York City? Why do you think he was missing Connecticut?

G. Do you think the Bellinis would have let Chester stay even if he refused to play? Were his musical abilities more important than his relationship with the family?

Vocabulary Exercise

Instructions

These are some words and phrases used in *The Cricket in Times Square*. Write each of their definition in English. Then, write a paragraph with the topic of your liking using <u>at least seven</u> of these words/phrases. Be mindful that one word/phrase can have multiple meanings or be used in more than one way. Carefully consider how the words and phrases were used in the original book, and try to use each word/phrase the same way as how the book used it.

Words & Phrases

exclaim	polite	rapidly	occasion	dumbfounded
remarkable	salvage	disgrace	imitate	insist

Sentences from the book

Here are the sentences from the original book that contains the given words and phrases. Only use these as reference and do not write the same sentences for your exercise.

exclaim: He peered down through the bars of the cricket cage and **exclaimed** with delight.

polite: Chester bowed back and gave one of his most **polite** chirps.

rapidly: He began talking **rapidly** in Chinese.

occasion: "… I have a heatproof, insulated bag saved up for just such an **occasion**."

dumbfounded: Mari was **dumbfounded**. He stared astonished at the cricket cage and then at his mother.

remarkable: And so began the most **remarkable** week in Chester Cricket's—or any cricket's—life.

salvage: They carted away all the hopelessly burned magazines and tried to **salvage** some that had only been scorched.

disgrace: So Chester started to chirp again. He was in such **disgrace** anyway, what difference could it make?

imitate & insist: Of course after such a sample of his talent for **imitating** songs, his friends **insisted** that he keep on.

Paragraph Write-up Exercise

Instructions

Write a short paragraph expressing your thoughts about the following questions. There are multiple questions to guide you arrange your thoughts and form your answer. Be sure to answer all the questions within a single paragraph—do not answer the questions individually.

A "paragraph" is a collection of sentences (which are not divided into separate lines) that convey a single idea throughout. The sentences in a paragraph must be logically arranged to coherently deliver your thoughts to the reader. A single paragraph must contain at least three sentences.

Question

How does music influence you? What do you think are the powers of music? Do you think music can serve as a form of communication between people with different languages and backgrounds?

Bibliography

George Selden Thompson (born May 14, 1929; died Dec 5, 1989, aged 60), known more by his pen name "George Selden," was an American children and young-adults' author born in Connecticut, U.S. *The Cricket in Times Square* remains to be his most recognized work, for which he produced six sequels afterward.

Other Books by the Author

Columns of each table: (from left) Title of Book; Year Published; ATOS Book Level; Lexile Measure; Interest Level.

Guide to Interest Level:

LG (Lower Grades; suitable for grades K-3)

MG (Middle Grades; suitable for grades 4-8)

MG+ (Middle Grades Plus; suitable for grades 6+)

UG (Upper Grades; suitable for grades 9-12)

Chester Cricket and His Friends Series				
Pertaining to *The Cricket in Time Square's* success, George Selden produced six sequels which all feature the same widely-loved characters: Chester Cricket, Tucker the Mouse, and Harry the Cat.				
The Cricket in Times Square *1961 Newbery Honor	1960	4.9	780L	MG
Tucker's Countryside	1969	4.9	750L	MG
Harry Cat's Pet Puppy	1974	4.8		MG
Chester Cricket's Pigeon Ride	1981	5.1	820L	MG
Chester Cricket's New Home	1983	4.6	740L	MG
Harry Kitten and Tucker Mouse	1986	4.0	600L	LG
The Old Meadow	1987	4.6		MG

Bud, Not Buddy

by Christopher Paul Curtis

Published	1999 (2000 Newbery Medal)
ATOS Book Level	5.0
Lexile	950L
Word Count	52179

Plot Introduction

Being left in the world alone without a single family member is a horrifying thought on its own. But imagine being a *ten-year-old kid* in the middle of *a nationwide economic crisis* without any kin. Our hero, Bud Caldwell, finds himself in this ludicrous predicament. Bud always knew his momma to be his only family, so he became self-reliant at six when she passed away. Since then, Bud grew up in an orphanage he calls "Home," which recently decided to close its doors due to financial struggles. Though four years have flown since his loss, Bud still cherishes vivid memories of his momma—especially the one that involves *the blue flyer*. The flyer contains a photo of a jazz band; in it, there is Herman E. Calloway—a man Bud is *convinced* is his father. Bud recalls his mother possessed many flyers of the band, yet she only turned hysterical on the one with Calloway. (Only the *blue* flyer displayed Calloway's face.) Kicked out of Home, Bud concludes that he has no choice but to find Calloway. Whether it's luck or sympathy, Bud receives lots of help from strangers on his journey—namely, he gets a free 120-mile ride from Lefty Lewis to reach the base camp of Calloway's band. Finally, Bud confronts the man and announces him as his father in front of all the other band members. But none of the members are convinced because Calloway never mentioned he had a son. Despite the haphazard claim, the band takes Bud in when they realize he's an orphan. It appears Bud will settle in among the band members and continue to live an abundant life. But there's yet a surprise waiting for him: Herman's real identity. Will Herman really turn out to be Bud's father?

Themes

Bud, Not Buddy is one of those books that involve rich historical contexts. The novel takes place in the United States during the 1930s—the decade when the Great Depression disheartened the country. As always, it is *your job* to research and study the historical background; I will only provide a brief summary here. First, let's rewind the clock a decade and look at the 1920s. During the 1920s, the US economy grew incredibly fast—its national wealth *doubled* between 1920 and 1929. Several factors contributed to this: first, the US obtained massive profit throughout World War I (1914-1918) from selling various military supplies to the belligerents; continued technological development also facilitated mass production of consumer goods in the US, which led to mass spending. Whenever a country's economy reaches for the clouds, so do its *stocks*. The US stock market thrived in the 1920s, and everyone—from millionaires to janitors—surrendered all their earnings to buy stocks. The market offered *guaranteed profit*—at massive margins too! It was stupid not to invest in stocks. However, experts eventually started noticing the volatility of the stocks. Of course, the US economy was doing great, but the stocks were doing *too great*. Mass production had slowed down, and unemployment had risen; meanwhile, amid increasing production, wages had remained low, and thus spending had declined. Yet the stock market was reaching for the stars—a massive *bubble* spawned in the stock market. This bubble popped on "Black Thursday" (October 24, 1929), when nervous investors started liquidating the overpriced stocks in massive numbers. Consequently, the stock prices plummeted to the ground. Some 12.9 million shares were traded that day—a record that was overturned right next Tuesday ("Black Tuesday"; October 29, 1929) when 16 million shares were traded. As a result, *nearly half* of the money that represented the stock market vanished into thin air. Individuals lost their life savings, consumer spending became non-existent, production stopped, people lost their jobs, individuals and companies could not pay back their debts, and the banks failed—the entire US economy went into chaos. The low point of the US economy continued for the next eleven years. I'll cut the story here and let you find out how the US recovered from the Great Depression on your own. But, hopefully, now you have a good idea of what the Great Depression was and how it began.

In the story, you can find several hints about the Great Depression: Bud's orphanage closing down, the mission providing free food to people, the "cardboard jungle" that is "Hooverville," Lefty Lewis talking about labor reforms and protests, etc.

Next, *Bud, Not Buddy* offers another fantastic opportunity to consider the concept of "*home.*" As we discussed in the previous chapter, we usually refer to the place we permanently live and/or that contains our family as our "home." Unfortunately, Bud doesn't have either of those—after he moves out of Home, Bud no longer has permanent residence nor knows any kin. But let's rewind a little further: Bud has never *felt* at home after losing his mother. This is because he has never been surrounded by people who love and care for him until he meets the band members. We noted how the *group of people* present might be a critical factor when considering a place your home. A place where you feel comfort, love, and security and have the right people to make you feel so is worthy of being your home. For Bud, this is precisely the band house.

Poverty is another marked theme in this book. Let's consider *how people act in poverty*. The Great Depression brought poverty to all; everyone was equally poor and dire during this period.

Interestingly, people tend to be more enthusiastic about helping each other during such universal hardship. We witness this in several instances of the book: Bud's "pretend parents" secure him a seat at the mission, and Lefty Lewis helps Bud reach Grand Rapids. When everyone bears the same struggles, people understand each other's situations precisely. And while you probably also require help, such comprehension encourages you to offer a helping hand. This does not only apply to economic distress—the same happens in the case of a war or a natural disaster. Though everyone suffers, they cooperate to escape from the suffering. Conversely, when there is no unifying predicament for everyone, we often observe selfish acts and ignorance. It *is* challenging to understand others' situations in the absence of a unifying hardship. But we should always try our best to understand each other's circumstances and offer as much help as we can.

Questions

① Summary and First Impressions

A. Can you describe your favorite part of the story? Why do you like the part the most?

B. What do you think about the story? Do you like it?

② Discussion Questions

A. Why do so many people gladly help Bud (even though they themselves are struggling) throughout the story?

> **Reminder**
>
> Bud receives help from many strangers throughout the story. First, the married couple waiting in line for free food at the mission—who Bud refers to as his "pretend parents"—helps Bud get his free meal, although he arrives too late to line up. Next, the large group of people in Hooverville around the campfire provides Bud with food and a place to sleep. Perhaps Bud receives the biggest help from Lefty Lewis, who gives him a free ride of over a hundred miles from Flint to Grand Rapids. In fact, the band members help Bud incredibly too—by taking him in and gifting him a new home.

    i.   Do you think people offer help to each other more readily if everyone is struggling with the same issue (like The Great Depression)? Why do people choose to help others when they are struggling as well?

    ii.   Do you think people help each other less under normal living conditions? Why do people not help each other if the majority is living struggle-free?

B. Why do you think so many people were trying to get on the train bound for Chicago at Hooverville? Why do you think the train left earlier than the schedule, and what do you think about how the police handled the situation?

> **Reminder**
>
> A train bound for Chicago was leaving the next morning of Bud arriving in Hooverville. However, Bud woke up the next day to someone yelling: "Get up, they're trying to sneak it out early!" Hundreds of men were trying to get on the train for free. Five policemen came, but four quickly gave up trying to stop the people.

C. Why do you think Bud believed so firmly that Herman E. Calloway was his father (even though he had never met him)? How did his mother react to the flyer containing Herman's photo? Why do you think she reacted to it in such a way?

D. On their way to Grand Rapids, Lefty and Bud meets a police officer looking for "labor organizers." Lefty mentions later that these labor organizers are trying to get unions in the automobile factories in Flint. Why do you think these events are happening, and why do you think the police wanted to catch the labor organizers?

E. What do you think Herman E. Calloway would have thought when he first received the telegram from Lefty? What do you think he would have thought when Bud announced that he was his father? Do you think he ever considered the possibility that he might be his grandson before he saw Bud's etched rocks?

F. Why do you think Bud finally felt like he was where he belonged when he was among the band members? How was the band's base camp different from all the other homes (e.g., Home—the orphanage, Amoses' house) Bud had experienced?

   i.   Do you think it really mattered to Bud that Herman was his grandfather (i.e., someone related to him in blood)? What if Herman turned out to have absolutely no relations to Bud? Do you think Bud would have still been happy to stay among the band members?

G. Which events indicate that there's an economic crisis (The Great Depression) going on? Why?

H. Why do you think the band members were comparatively rich than the general public?

   i.   This was actually true during The Great Depression—musical bands and their members were some of the richest people during this era. Why do you think musical bands did so well during the depression? Why was entertainment so important during those times?

Vocabulary Exercise

These are some words and phrases used in *Bud, Not Buddy*. Write each of their definition in English. Then, write a paragraph with the topic of your liking using <u>at least seven</u> of these words/phrases. Be mindful that one word/phrase can have multiple meanings or be used in more than one way. Carefully consider how the words and phrases were used in the original book, and try to use each word/phrase the same way as how the book used it.

Words & Phrases

privilege	considerate	retrieve	headfirst	practical
dodge	remind	devour	unusual	
catch [*person/people*]'s breath				

Sentences from the book

Here are the sentences from the original book that contains the given words and phrases. Only use these as reference and do not write the same sentences for your exercise.

privilege: "... You think you got some kind of special **privilege** just 'cause you're skinny and raggedy?"

considerate: ... please be **considerate** and patient ...

retrieve: "... Would you like to **retrieve** your suitcase?"

headfirst: If a grown-up ever starts a sentence by saying "haven't you heard," get ready, 'cause what's about to come out of their mouth is gonna drop you **headfirst** into a boiling tragedy.

practical: "Fifty-four hours! Much too long to be **practical**."

dodge: "So? That's better than being cold and hungry all the time and **dodging** the railroad police."

remind: And that smell always reminded me of Momma and how she used to read me to sleep every night.

devour: "I am really impressed, you really **devoured** that book, didn't you?"

unusual: "Now there's an **unusual** name. Did you run away from home, Bud-not-Buddy?"

catch [*person/people*]'s breath: I sat on the side of the tracks and tried to **catch my breath**.

Paragraph Write-up Exercise

Instructions

Write a short paragraph expressing your thoughts about the following questions. There are multiple questions to guide you arrange your thoughts and form your answer. Be sure to answer all the questions within a single paragraph—do not answer the questions individually.

A "paragraph" is a collection of sentences (which are not divided into separate lines) that convey a single idea throughout. The sentences in a paragraph must be logically arranged to coherently deliver your thoughts to the reader. A single paragraph must contain at least three sentences.

Question

What is your definition of 'home'? Between the location of your home and the people at your home, which side matters more to you? Do you think it is possible for you to have more than one 'home'?

Bibliography

1 – "Great Depression History" from *History.com* (https://www.history.com/topics/great-depression/great-depression-history)

2 – "Hard Times in Illinois, 1930-1940) from *The Official Website for the Illinois Secretary of State* (https://www.ilsos.gov/departments/archives/teaching_packages/hard_times/home.html)

About the Author

Christopher Paul Curtis (69, born May 10, 1953) is an American children and young-adults' author born in Michigan, U.S. He specializes on historical fiction and prefers following his characters' narratives rather than the overall plot. His most well-known works include *Bud, Not Buddy*, *The Watsons Go to Birmingham – 1963*, and *Elijah of Buxton*.

https://nobodybutcurtis.com/biography

Other Books by the Author

Columns of each table: (from left) Title of Book; Year Published; ATOS Book Level; Lexile Measure; Interest Level.

Guide to Interest Level:

LG (Lower Grades; suitable for grades K-3)

MG (Middle Grades; suitable for grades 4-8)

MG+ (Middle Grades Plus; suitable for grades 6+)

UG (Upper Grades; suitable for grades 9-12)

Flint Future Detectives Club Series				
Mr. Chickee's Funny Money	2005	5.3	890L	MG
Mr. Chickee's Messy Mission	2007	5.6	870L	MG

Novels				
The Watsons Go to Birmingham - 1963 *1996 Newbery Honor	1995	5.0	920L	MG
Bud, Not Buddy *2000 Newbery Medal	1999	5.0	950L	MG
Bucking the Sarge	2004	5.8	1000L	MG
Elijah of Buxton *2008 Newbery Honor	2007	5.4	980L	MG
The Mighty Miss Malone	2012	4.7	750L	MG
The Madman of Piney Woods	2014	5.7	870L	MG
The Journey of Little Charlie	2018	5.8	960L	MG

Mrs. Frisby and the Rats of NIMH

by Robert C. O'Brien

Published	1971 (1972 Newbery Medal)
ATOS Book Level	5.1
Lexile	790L
Word Count	53752

Plot Introduction

Have you ever wondered how intelligent rats can get? According to this book—given the right treatment—rats can learn to read and write in English and mimic high-level human technology. Our heroine, Mrs. Frisby, is a recently-widowed rat living on a farmer's field. Right from the get-go, things are not looking up—her son, Timothy, is suffering from a severe illness, and there's only a little time remaining until the plowing. With spring coming back, farmer Fitzgibbon is preparing to plow his field; Mrs. Frisby and her children must relocate to their summerhouse before he begins, or else they'll get hurt. Unfortunately, Timothy is not looking healthy enough for the move. Mrs. Frisby seeks advice from a wise owl, who directs her to a rat colony near her home. Mrs. Frisby is astonished when she visits them, for they possess advanced human technology—including electricity, elevators, and light bulbs. The leader of the colony, Nicodemus, is hesitant to help Mrs. Frisby until he hears her name. It turns out Mrs. Frisby's deceased husband, Jonathan Frisby, was captured along with Nicodemus in a research foundation called The National Institute of Mental Health (NIMH). There, rats and mice were administered experimental shots that granted them the ability to read and write in English. One day, the rats obtained the instructions to their cages, which they deciphered with ease, thanks to their medication. They managed to open their cage doors and escaped the lab. While some decided to return to their original lives, others built a new civilization. They adopted human technology by reading manuals; now, they plan to achieve self-sustainability by learning how to farm, so they can stop stealing from humans. Will Mrs. Frisby safely escape with her children, and will Nicodemus accomplish his ultimate goal?

Themes

Mrs. Frisby and the Rats of NIMH presents the perfect opportunity to discuss *animal experiments*. Every year, hundreds of millions of animals are subjected to countless scientific experiments; more than 100 million are estimated to be killed during the process. Various species are sacrificed for diverse purposes. Principally, rats and mice are used frequently in medical tests and brain research—they bear high levels of similarities to humans in their anatomy and genes. (Apparently, we share over 95% of genes with rats and mice.) Next, rabbits are often used for cosmetics testing—especially eye and skin products. Rabbits do not possess tear ducts, so they do not "cry out" foreign substances from their eyes. This allows the observation of the long-term effects of eye products. Many other species—including frogs, dogs, cats, hamsters, guinea pigs, monkeys, fish, and birds—are used for animal experiments.

This raises an ethical concern: *is it okay to use animals for such tests?* Of course, it's *not*. Not only can the experiments hurt or kill the animals, but the set-up and preparation alone can also torture them. Many test subjects are confined to cramped spaces and given minimal food before the experiments to reduce maintenance costs. Furthermore, depending on the characteristics of the study, some animals must stay restrained in painful positions and postures for hours. Taking the rabbit as an example, rabbits are reportedly constrained firmly during eye cosmetics tests to avoid them wiping their eyes. Unfortunately, there's another problem: animal experiments are essential in some areas, and there are no satisfactory alternatives. This is particularly true for medicinal research. When developing a new drug or a formula, it's paramount to ensure no side effects, if not minimal. More than the drug working as intended, it must not cause any serious adverse effects. We cannot test fresh-off-of-design drugs directly on humans as they might harm or even kill them—that's why we use animals instead. Every new drug undergoes exhaustive, repeated testing until its safety is guaranteed. That's why it takes so long until a new drug reaches the shelf.

Lastly, the validity of animal test results is also debatable. Sometimes, animal experiments may fail to provide the correct picture—the effects of the product may differ when a human uses it compared to, say, a rat. A famous example regarding this argument is the catastrophic case of "thalidomide." Thalidomide gained attention due to its ability to cure morning sickness in pregnant women. Thalidomide was tested on various species, and it was concluded that a lethal dose of the drug practically did not exist. Following the animal test results, the medicine was regarded as safe for humans and was approved for use in many countries throughout the mid-1950s. Unfortunately, the scientists did not realize *the drug could affect the baby in the womb*. Until thalidomide was cut from the market in 1962, the drug is estimated to have damaged over 10,000 newborns, killing roughly half of them within months from birth while leaving permanent defects on the survivors. This disaster provided the much-needed epiphany in the medical industry that animal tests should never be blindly trusted. I'll halt the discussion about animal experiments here; there's lots of information on animal experiments out there. I'll leave you to search and consider the details yourself.

Away from animal experiments, this book also allows us to consider *the power of the human language*. In the book, Nicodemus and "the rats of NIMH" were able to achieve incredible levels of technology thanks to being taught how to read and write in English. (Well, right off the bat, they escaped from the laboratory thanks to this.) So, how does the human language compare to the animal language, and what does the difference grant us? It is said that the most striking difference between the human language and the animal (more so) "communication" is whether the signal is *abstract* or *concrete*—pointing to a cat would be a *concrete* signal while saying the word "cat" would be an *abstract* signal. While humans are capable of both forms of signaling, animals are believed to be only capable of the *concrete* type. If you think about it, the word "cat" has nothing to do with the animal. However, we understand what someone is trying to say when they vocalize the word "cat." Animals cannot perform this kind of communication—they cannot share ideas in an *abstract* fashion. This distinctly sets apart how humans and animals *think*. Only humans can consider abstract concepts like *justice*, *mercy*, and *relationships*. And this is why we have much more advanced technology than animals. Humans, unlike animals, can consider abstract concepts, ideas, and plans to seek and implement improvements in various areas of their lives.

Questions

① Summary and First Impressions

A. Can you describe your favorite part of the story? Why do you like the part the most?

B. What do you think about the story? Do you like it?

② Discussion Questions

A. Why do you think the scientists use animals for their experiments (i.e., for research purposes)? Why do you think they don't use humans as their test subjects (even though their goal is to develop products for humans)?

B. Where do you think scientists use animal experiments (i.e., to study about or create what)?

C. Rats and mice are two of the most frequently used species in animal testing. Why do you think we use them so much? What advantages do they have compared to other animals (in science experiments)?

> ### Hint
>
> The rat and the mice's small sizes offer several perks compared to larger animals. Consider handling a tiger or a gorilla for an experiment. In addition, the volumes of most medical administrations scale with body weight—for example, if a child takes one pill a day, an adult would have to take two or three pills. Next, think of how rats breed. Scientists need to breed their own test subjects in the laboratory. More prolific and fast-reproducing species would be preferable. Also, consider if rats and mice bear any physiological or biological similarities to humans.

D. What other species do you think are used for animal experiments? Do you know a particular species that is used for a particular purpose?

E. Do you think it is okay to use animals for science research? Let's consider the ethics/morals of using animals for experiments.

    i. If we can guarantee that the animal subjects will not die (but will suffer), is it okay?

    ii. Does it depend on the species? Is it okay to perform experiments on some species but not on the others?

F. Now, let's look at it from the opposite perspective. Are animals truly effective test subjects for developing medicines, therapies, cosmetics, etc. for humans? Can we always trust the validity of animal test results? Are the effects and side effects (of a certain product) the same on animals as humans?

G. If you think animal experiments have problems (either in their ethics or legitimacy, or both), what are the alternatives?

    i.   Is it okay to administer newly developed drugs, formulas, products, etc. on humans directly without any testing?

    ii.   If not, then, how can we test a newly developed product without using animals?

H. Do you think learning to read and write was ultimately more positive or negative to the rats? Do you think Nicodemus and the other rats benefitted overall from learning to read and write?

    i.   If the rats had never learned how to read and write, do you think they would have been happy in their cages? Do you think they would have not wished to escape?

    ii.   Learning to read and write made the rats of NIMH smarter—they could utilize some of the human technologies. However, this made them outcast from the rest of the rats in the world. Nicodemus's colony is a small bunch that can no longer mix with the other rats. Weighing the pro and con, do you think this transformation was truly worth for the rats of NIMH?

    iii.   When Nicodemus proposed "The Plan," not every rat was optimistic about it. Especially, Jenner refused to follow his friend's ambitious scheme. Why do you think he gave up on it? Could it be related to the previous question?

> ### Chew on this
>
> After Nicodemus, his friend Jenner, and the other rats escaped from NIMH, Nicodemus suggested The Plan, which was his ambitious scheme to become completely independent of humans. More specifically, Nicodemus intended to build an entirely self-reliant colony that no longer needed to steal from humans. This charming plot, interestingly, failed to convince all the escapees—Jenner and a few other rats decided to drop the plan and go their own way. The reason for the rejection is never disclosed, but perhaps they felt that rats should not enjoy a such level of technology, or they thought that The Plan was too difficult for mere rats to achieve.

I. What do you think was the goal of the scientists' experiments at NIMH? What injection formula do you think they were trying to develop?

> **Chew on this**
>
> The injections the rats of NIMH received granted them the ability to read and write. Who and what do you think the injections were for? Do you think the scientists were developing the formula for humans? What do you think would happen if a human—who can already read and write—received the injections? Would they make them smarter? Or do you think the scientists were simply curious if they could develop a cure that will make rats and mice more intelligent?

    i.   Do you think the scientists should have expected the consequences (i.e., the rats escaping from the lab)? Do you think they were a bit careless?

J. Capable of speaking human's language, Nicodemus and his fellow rats could incorporate human technologies—such as electricity, lightbulbs, and elevators—to their lair (by reading books and relevant materials). How does our language allow us to be more advanced than animals? How come none of the other species have any technology even remotely close to ours?

    i.   How has reading changed you? How would you be different if you hadn't read as much as you have so far?

Vocabulary Exercise

Instructions

These are some words and phrases used in *Mrs. Frisby and the Rats of NIMH*. Write each of their definition in English. Then, write a paragraph with the topic of your liking using <u>at least seven</u> of these words/phrases. Be mindful that one word/phrase can have multiple meanings or be used in more than one way. Carefully consider how the words and phrases were used in the original book, and try to use each word/phrase the same way as how the book used it.

Words & Phrases

doubt	relentless	eventually	sympathetic r	oundabout (*adj.*)
resemble	temptation	senseless	absently (*adv.*),	accompanied by

Sentences from the book

Here are the sentences from the original book that contains the given words and phrases. Only use these as reference and do not write the same sentences for your exercise.

doubt: She **doubted** it; surely, if he had such medicine he would have given it to her the first time.

relentless: … and since the cat stalked those grounds **relentlessly**, she had to plot a much more roundabout way, circling the whole wide farmyard.

eventually: "You can see what this would have been a dreadful thing for Jonathan to have to tell you … He would have told you **eventually** …"

sympathetic: So he clucked **sympathetically** when he heard Mrs. Frisby's story …

roundabout: She could go home by the same **roundabout** way she had come, in which case she would surely end up walking alone in the woods in the dark …

resemble: Mr. Ages' house, somewhat larger than a shoebox but about the same shape, **resembled** the house of a hermit.

temptation: "… If this case is still open, with the machines and lights, …, there will be a terrible **temptation** to give up and move back to the soft life."

senseless: … and after looking at me in surprise, they both scurried up an oak tree and scolded **senselessly** in loud voices …

absently (*adv.*): No one had noticed the small torn piece of paper at first; then Mrs. Fitzgibbon had **absently** picked it up and tossed it into the wastebasket.

accompanied by: … the sound of hunters' guns shooting, the sound that is **accompanied**, for someone, **by** a fiery stabbing pain.

Paragraph Write-up Exercise

Instructions

Write a short paragraph expressing your thoughts about the following questions. There are multiple questions to guide you arrange your thoughts and form your answer. Be sure to answer all the questions within a single paragraph—do not answer the questions individually.

A "paragraph" is a collection of sentences (which are not divided into separate lines) that convey a single idea throughout. The sentences in a paragraph must be logically arranged to coherently deliver your thoughts to the reader. A single paragraph must contain at least three sentences.

Question

What do you think about using animals like rats for science experiments? Say that we can save one person by sacrificing one rat. Is this a fair trade?

Bibliography

1 – "Facts and Statistics About Animal Testing" from *People for the Ethical Treatment of Animals (PETA)* (https://www.peta.org/issues/animals-used-for-experimentation/animals-used-experimentation-factsheets/animal-experiments-overview/)

2 – "FACTS AND FIGURES ON ANIMAL TESTING" from *Cruelty Free International* (https://crueltyfreeinternational.org/about-animal-testing/facts-and-figures-animal-testing)

3 – "Rabbits: Blinded for Beauty" from *Humane Society International* (https://www.hsi.org/news-media/blinded_rabbits/)

4 – "THALIDOMIDE" from *Science Museum* (https://www.sciencemuseum.org.uk/objects-and-stories/medicine/thalidomide)

About the Author

Robert Leslie Carrol Conly (born Jan 11, 1918; died Mar 5, 1973, aged 55), known more by his pen name, "Robert C. O'Brien," was an American science-fiction author and journalist for *National Geographic* magazine born in New York, U.S. He began his writing career in the 1960s when he contracted glaucoma and could no longer continue his journalism career. He has produced a total of four books and is most well-known for *Mrs. Frisby and the Rats of NIMH* and *Z for Zachariah*. (The latter was apparently intended for adults.)

Other Books by the Author

Columns of each table: (from left) Title of Book; Year Published; ATOS Book Level; Lexile Measure; Interest Level.

Guide to Interest Level:
LG (Lower Grades; suitable for grades K-3)
MG (Middle Grades; suitable for grades 4-8)
MG+ (Middle Grades Plus; suitable for grades 6+)
UG (Upper Grades; suitable for grades 9-12)

Novels				
The Silver Crown	1968	5.2	790L	MG
Mrs. Frisby and the Rats of NIMH *1972 Newbery Medal	1971	5.1	790L	MG

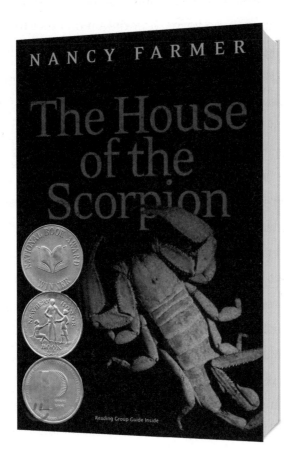

The House of the Scorpion

by Nancy Farmer

Published	2002 (2003 Newbery Honor)
ATOS Book Level	5.1
Lexile	660L
Word Count	100214

Plot Introduction

Have you ever wished for *eternal life*? It sure sounds tempting, but humanity is far from acquiring it yet. In this book, however, your dream comes true. Opium is an imaginary future country under the reign of the abusive drug lord, El Patrón. He has perfected *human cloning* technology which grants eternal life to himself and his family. Here's how it works: everyone in the family creates a personal clone; the clone is raised until it can yield mature, healthy organs; the original person replaces their worn-out organs with the clone's, which extends their lifespan. Our hero is Matt, the clone of El Patrón; at Matt's birth, his tyrant counterpart had already passed 140! Matt spends his first six years in a secluded house under the care of Celia, El Patrón's cook. He is discovered by three children—Steven, Emilia, and María—and is summoned to El Patrón's mansion. There, he meets El Patrón himself, who orders everyone to treat Matt with respect; he also grants Matt his own room, a bodyguard, and education. As Matt settles in the mansion, he gradually discovers his fate and realizes that clones like him are generally not welcomed. One day, El Patrón gets a heart attack, and Matt gets shipped to a hospital. Moments before his heart gets extracted, Celia announces that she has secretly fed Matt small doses of arsenic—a deadly poison. While the amount doesn't faze Matt, it could potentially be fatal to El Patrón's old body. Unable to receive the transplant, El Patrón dies, and Opium goes under lockdown. Only Matt can override it with his DNA identical to El Patrón's. Now, Matt must rise as the new leader of Opium and cleanse the country of El Patrón's sins.

Themes

The House of the Scorpion offers the perfect opportunity to discuss *cloning*. Cloning is not a brand-new concept—it has existed for decades. Amphibians were cloned as early as the 1950s, and even the first mammal was successfully cloned in 1996 (Dolly the Sheep). Better yet, you have probably consumed cloned produce before in one way or the other. Many varieties of apples, grapes, bananas, pears, peaches, potatoes, garlic, and blueberries you eat are *clones*. The agricultural industry actively practices cloning to enhance the quality of the products and facilitate the cultivation process. Plants and animals bearing favorable traits are cloned to preserve their valuable genes. Say you have the *ideal* dairy cow with a sizable udder. The girl has triumphantly yielded tremendous volumes of high-quality milk over many years. Unfortunately, an unknown condition forbids the precious girl from bearing any offspring. With time relentlessly ticking by, you fear you might have to say goodbye to her soon. Here, you can clone the cow to preserve all her glorious genes. By cloning animals with exceptional genes and selectively breeding the superior specimens, we can spread the favorable gene(s) quickly throughout the herd. For animals like cows, anything from their body sizes to producing high-quality milk and meat can be reasons to clone the animal. But the cloning of mammals is neither easy nor cheap. It would be impractical to clone superior specimens over and over again to acquire good produce. Instead, as stated, we combine cloning with selective breeding—we clone desirable specimens and preserve their priceless genes, then encourage them to breed. Nature will do the rest.

To allow a comprehensive discussion of human cloning, we must first investigate how we clone mammals. In particular, we will examine the case of Dolly the Sheep—the first mammal ever cloned. First, a donor cell was taken from the "original" *Dolly* (an adult female Finn-Dorset sheep), from which the *nucleus* (i.e., the part of a cell that contains all the genetic information) was separated. The nucleus was then *fused* with an *egg cell* (i.e., the female reproductive cell that had its nucleus removed—an emptied vessel for the nucleus), which had been extracted from an adult female Scottish Blackface sheep. The fused cell was then exposed to an electric pulse that stimulated its division. Once it had divided enough, the cell bunch was inserted into the womb of another adult female Scottish Blackface sheep (this one is called the "surrogate mother"). There, it grew into a baby sheep and was delivered. The sheep thus born had a white face like a Finn-Dorset, even though it received an egg cell from and was delivered by Scottish Blackface sheep (which, as the name suggests, had black faces); this confirmed the successful cloning of Dolly.

Humans, as mammals, can be cloned the same way as Dolly the Sheep. However, there are serious ethical concerns related to cloning humans. (No official record of human cloning exists so far.) Let's return to Dolly's case. As explained, cloning a single sheep requires the sacrifice of two adult female sheep—the first has to provide its egg cell, while the second has to get pregnant with and give birth to the cloned specimen. Putting this into perspective, we would require the sacrifice of two adult women to clone a single human being. This evidently jeopardizes women's right to have their own babies through natural reproduction. Next, the chances of successfully introducing the fused and divided cell into the surrogate mother's womb are profoundly low. The cell is an apparent lifeform: a failure at this stage could be perceived as a loss of life. The ethical concerns do not only lie in the cloning process. Cloning of desired human genes and selectively combining them in an attempt to create "improved humans" clearly infringes on human dignity, freedom, and equality.

However, we *do* apply cloning technology to humans in real life. In fact, cloning is a crucial part of powerful clinical therapies. But we just established there are serious ethical concerns about cloning humans. How is it okay to use it for medical processes? The point is: it's okay as long as you don't go the "full length" (i.e., until you get the baby). Then, how *do* we use cloning technology in medicine? We use the *cells* we acquire during the process. Let's consider Dolly's cloning process again. Once we get the fused cell, the cell starts dividing (with the correct treatment). If provided the appropriate environment (i.e., a womb), the dividing cell will eventually develop into a baby. This means—under the right conditions—the cell will divide to form all the internal organs (e.g., the intestines, liver, lungs, heart) and external body parts (e.g., the eyes, ears, mouth, nose, arms, hands). The cells we encounter at the early stage of cloning can develop into *any part* of the body. Hence, we can use these cells to *repair* any part of our bodies.

We call this: "stem cell" therapy. We apply the same initial steps as how Dolly was cloned. First, a nucleus is collected from a person's skin cell and is fused with an egg cell donated by an adult woman. The fused cell is then subjected to an environment where it can readily divide. Here, instead of inserting the cell bunch into a woman's body, it is ruptured to collect the "stem cells" inside. The stem cells are then cultivated in the lab until they are administered to the original person's injured body part.

What's fascinating about stem cells is not only do they grow into any body part, but they can also *recognize* the part they're attached to. When placed on a damaged body part, stem cells will *realize* which part they're on and quickly transform into cells required for that part. The crucial point, however, is that they need to be *your* stem cells—using someone else's stem cells to treat your injury not only has low chances of success but could also trigger extreme immune responses, which may worsen the damage.

Stem cell therapy proves particularly effective when treating *internal organ damage*. We are generally incapable of repairing our internal organs when damaged—the human body lacks the ability to develop cells to repair our organs. When your organ gets severely damaged, you only have two options: 1) to receive an organ transplant or 2) to receive stem cell therapy. An organ transplant may be cheaper (not by a large margin), but healthy, compatible organs are not always available. Hence is why stem cell therapy is critical to internal organ damage repair.

Theoretically, stem cell therapy is the perfect way to heal any injury—whether inside or outside your body, your stem cells will automatically learn which body part they're on and quickly propagate to heal the wound. However, there's one problem: stem cell therapy is *extremely expensive*. Ensuring success in every step toward acquiring stem cells—the extraction of the nucleus, the fusion, the division, the handling of stem cells, etc.—is *incredibly difficult*. Stem cell therapy is not something you get prescribed to treat your falling-off-of-a-bicycle-and-scraping-your-arm injury. Realistically, only those with *no other choice* (often cancer patients) receive stem cell therapy. Perhaps one day we shall achieve the universal application of this almighty technology, but alas.

Okay, that was a deep discussion about cloning. Other than that, there aren't many big topics to talk about in this book. One could be the *abusive nature* of El Patrón. El Patrón is quite a *vicious* leader. He is unforgiving to those who try to get in his way of achieving his desires. We see throughout the book that his violent nature damages various parts of Opium—having such an abusive leader can lead to numerous problems. But once someone seizes such a status, it could be challenging to bring them down. Therefore, we should carefully consider who can handle the responsibility before something like that happens. And we should evaluate how much power is *too much*. For these concerns, modern politics places several facilities and committees that keep one's power in check. And this is also why many countries have multiple political "parties"—to constantly keep each other in check.

Questions

① Summary and First Impressions

A. Can you describe your favorite part of the story? Why do you like the part the most?

B. What do you think about the story? Do you like it?

② Discussion Questions

A. What do you think about the clones in the book? Do you consider them equivalent to humans? Should we treat them just like how we treat normal humans? Do they deserve such respect?

> **Hint**
>
> Perhaps it helps to consider Matt separately from the eejit-turned clones.

B. How does Matt think about himself after he realizes he's a clone? How would you feel if you turned out to be a clone of someone else?

C. Matt is El Patrón's clone, but they are not 100% the same. How are they different?

> **Chew on this**
>
> Being a clone of someone else would mean you have identical genes to your original copy. However, not all human's traits—appearances, personalities, talents, etc.—are determined by their genes. A person's environment (i.e., living conditions) also has a substantial influence on shaping one's character. Now, consider Matt and El Patrón. How are their living conditions different? How was El Patrón's childhood different from Matt's right now? How would such a difference affect their traits? For one, what is a talent that Matt has while El Patrón doesn't? Also, how are their personalities and thought processes different?

D. Why do you think El Patrón treats Matt so nicely, even though he is well aware that he will eventually take Matt's life to extend his own?

   i.   Why do you think El Patrón gives Matt his own room and a bodyguard?

   ii.   Why do you think El Patrón provides Matt education?

E. Do you think it's fair for certain people (like the leaders of countries, organizations, companies etc.) to possess higher power than others?

   i.   Can one have *too much* power?

F. Does power allow someone to do whatever they want? Can people of power get away with doing whatever they want?

G. What do you think about El Patrón's abusive nature? How does his power affect the people of Opium?

   i.   What could be the problems of having such a vicious leader in real life?

   ii.   What do you think we can do to prevent people like El Patrón appearing today?

H. What is your opinion on cloning? Do you think it has more positive effects or negative effects? Do you think cloning should be allowed?

   i.   Why do you think people would want to clone of themselves? Where do you think they would use their clones?

   ii.   If you could create your clone right now, would you? If so, why, and if not, why not?

   iii.   If you were to create your clone, which similarities do you think he/she would share with you? What would be the differences?

I. Let's now think about the ethics of cloning. Do you think it's okay for someone to create their clone? Do you think it's okay for someone to use their clone for whichever purpose they desire?

i. How much right and dignity does a human clone deserve? Should they be treated the same as an authentic human being?

J. What problems (other than ethics) do you think cloning possesses? If cloning were allowed, how would it impact humanity as a whole?

K. Consider the cloning of Dolly the Sheep (consult the *Themes* section). Between the first female (who provides the egg cell) and the second female (the "surrogate mother," i.e., the one who gives birth to the clone), who deserves the custody of the clone? Who is the real mother?

L. Consider stem cell therapy (consult the *Themes* section). Once the nucleus from your skin cell and a donated egg cell are fused, we have a life. Following the appropriate steps, the fused cell can grow into a full-on baby. However, we rupture the blastocyst to harvest the contained cells instead. While a blastocyst looks very different from a human baby, the successful introduction of it into a woman's womb will allow it to grow into one. Then, is rupturing the blastocyst killing a lifeform (i.e., murder)? Is a blastocyst too early to be called a lifeform?

Vocabulary Exercise

Instructions

These are some words and phrases used in *The House of the Scorpion*. Write each of their definition in English. Then, write a paragraph with the topic of your liking using <u>at least seven</u> of these words/phrases. Be mindful that one word/phrase can have multiple meanings or be used in more than one way. Carefully consider how the words and phrases were used in the original book, and try to use each word/phrase the same way as how the book used it.

Words & Phrases

criticize	hostile	abomination	accuse	demand
confront	sacrifice	frantically	nauseous	maneuver

Sentences from the book

Here are the sentences from the original book that contains the given words and phrases. Only use these as reference and do not write the same sentences for your exercise.

criticize: Rosa stood in the hallway, watching and **criticizing**.

hostile: They were wary but not **hostile**. In fact, they behaved a lot like Tam Lin.

abomination: "… I wanted to *kill* that **abomination** El Patrón keeps at his heels." Matt felt cold. He'd had no idea how much Felicia hated him.

accuse: … and afterward invited the boys to confess sins. And every night the boys, led by Ton-Ton, hurled **accusations** at Matt. It was meant to humiliate him …

demand: At least once a week Matt dreamed of the dead man in the field … He was terribly, horribly thirsty … It got so bad that Matt **demanded** a pitcher of water by his <u>bed.</u>

confront: When he reached the end of the valley, he was **confronted** by a high granite cliff.

sacrifice: Matt thought she would easily **sacrifice** him to realize her goal.

frantically: Fidelito **frantically** scratched his lemon and held it to Mattson's nose.

nauseous: A slight breeze blew the **nauseous** stench of the river away, and Matt collapsed with his chest heaving.

maneuver: He **maneuvered** the machine as delicately a s a surgeon performing an operation.

Paragraph Write-up Exercise

Instructions

Write a short paragraph expressing your thoughts about the following questions. There are multiple questions to guide you arrange your thoughts and form your answer. Be sure to answer all the questions within a single paragraph—do not answer the questions individually.

A "paragraph" is a collection of sentences (which are not divided into separate lines) that convey a single idea throughout. The sentences in a paragraph must be logically arranged to coherently deliver your thoughts to the reader. A single paragraph must contain at least three sentences.

Question

If you were to create your own clone, what attributes (e.g., looks, personalities) would he/she have in common with you, and which ones would be different? If you could create your own clone right now, would you do so? Explain why (or why not).

Bibliography

1 – "Myths about Cloning" from *U.S. Food and Drug Administration* (https://www.fda.gov/animal-veterinary/animal-cloning/myths-about-cloning)

2 – "Eating Tasty Clones" from *Reason Magazine* (https://reason.com/2003/11/06/eating-tasty-clones/)

3 – "A Primer on Cloning and Its Use in Livestock Operations" from *U.S. Food and Drug Administration* (https://www.fda.gov/animal-veterinary/animal-cloning/primer-cloning-and-its-use-livestock-operations#interest)

4 – "The Story of Dolly" from *Ask A Biologist (Arizona State University)*

(https://askabiologist.asu.edu/content/story-dolly)

5 – "cloning: Ethical controversy" from *Encyclopedia Britannica*
(https://www.britannica.com/science/cloning/Ethical-controversy)

6 – "Stem cells: past, present, and future" from W. Zakrzewski et al. in *Stem Cell Research & Therapy* (https://stemcellres.biomedcentral.com/articles/10.1186/s13287-019-1165-5)

About the Author

Nancy Farmer (81; born 1941) is an American author born in Arizona, U.S. Her specialty is science-fiction fantasy novels for children and young adults. Her most well-known works include *The House of the Scorpion*, *The Ear, the Eye, and the Arm*, and *A Girl Named Disaster*.

https://www.nancyfarmerwebsite.com/

Other Books by the Author

Columns of each table: (from left) Title of Book; Year Published; ATOS Book Level; Lexile Measure; Interest Level.

Guide to Interest Level:
LG (Lower Grades; suitable for grades K-3)
MG (Middle Grades; suitable for grades 4-8)
MG+ (Middle Grades Plus; suitable for grades 6+)
UG (Upper Grades; suitable for grades 9-12)

House of the Scorpion Series				
The House of the Scorpion *2003 Newbery Honor	2002	5.1	660L	MG+
The Lord of Opium	2013	5.2	HL700L	MG+

Sea of Trolls Series				
The Sea of Trolls	2004	4.7	670L	MG

The Land of the Silver Apples	2007	5.0	710L	MG
The Islands of the Blessed	2009	5.4	730L	MG

Novels				
The Ear, The Eye, and the Arm *1995 Newbery Honor	1994	4.7	660L	UG
The Warm Place	1995	4.3	600L	MG
A Girl Named Disaster *1997 Newbery Honor	1996	5.1	730L	UG

Hatchet

by Gary Paulsen

Published	1987 (1988 Newbery Honor)
ATOS Book Level	5.7
Lexile	1020L
Word Count	42328

Being stranded alone in the wild is perhaps an overused cliché—many books (e.g., *Robinson Crusoe*), movies (e.g., *Casted Away*), and video games (e.g., *The Forest*) have employed it time and time again. However, no other artwork probes the survivalist's mind so brilliantly as *Hatchet*. Our hero is Brian Robeson, a thirteen-year-old boy who lives in New York City. Brian's parents are divorced; as the story begins, he boards a plane to visit his father in Canada. The passengers are only him and the pilot. Still far from the destination, the pilot suffers a heart attack, and Brian is left alone to steer the plane. Luckily, he manages to land it in a lake and survives the crash. Thus begins Brian's fifty-four-day survival challenge in the wild. At first, Brian prepares a crude home inside a hollow rock and relies on easy-to-gather food (such as berries and turtle eggs). He foolishly believes rescue will arrive soon, and he only has to survive a few days. But he soon realizes that blind hope is not going to get him anywhere. Brian starts searching for more sustainable and nutritious food sources; he teaches himself how to make fire; he continuously upgrades his arsenal and shelter. Throughout the process, he experiences a fair share of failure—like eating poisonous berries and upsetting a skunk—and frustration—like missing a passing-by plane and having his shelter destroyed by a tornado—but he carries on. He views his mistakes as learning opportunities and grows more resilient by the day. His focus is no longer on getting rescued—it is simply on surviving another day. Then, one day, he recovers an emergency transmitter from the sunken plane that can broadcast his location. Will Brian finally get rescued and return to civilization?

Themes

Hatchet is all about *transformation*. Brian transforms in many ways throughout his astonishing journey in the forest. As hinted above, at the core of his transformations lies the maturing of his mind. At first, Brian put forward blind hope that he would be rescued soon; he only focused on surviving the instant and avoiding immediate dangers. However, he soon realizes he should seriously take on some long-term planning. His rescue didn't arrive as quickly as he had hoped for, and he realized he might have to survive a lot longer than he had initially anticipated. At the same time, Brian stopped feeling sorry for himself; he stopped being unduly wounded over unfortunate events. At the beginning of his survival, he got broken over some tart berries making him ill—but later in the book, he stayed virtually indifferent even after getting his ribs destroyed by a charging moose and his home blown away by a tornado. Brian also used to be devastated at the simplest mistakes—such as failing to hunt—but he soon started perceiving his mistakes as learning opportunities. This attitude made him no longer shy of mistakes but rather welcoming. Brian grows tough and self-sustained throughout his days in the wild. Thankfully, he carries these changes over to the city—he maintains a relaxed, appreciative attitude throughout his life. Brian definitely turned out differently after his journey.

Here's something else about Brian that transforms: his *wisdom*. The longer he survives and the more he makes mistakes, the more he learns and adapts. At first, everything was foreign— Brian didn't understand why wild animals acted in some ways and why the wild was changing in some ways. He was dumbfounded when he first met the bear, who did not care about him at all. Through careful observation, Brian teaches himself many valuable things—especially about *the ways of the wild*. He realized that wild animals do not show aggression unless provoked, except for when their cubs are present; he studied the movements of the fishes and the birds to become virtually error-free in his hunting; he realized that fire could double as heat and protection. The change in his attitude explained in the preceding paragraph also helped a lot, as he would have never learned anything from his mistakes unless he changed his mindset.

Here are some other bite-sized transformations to consider. In the beginning, Brian was obsessed with his unfortunate family situation—this made him linger in the *past*. But, while surviving in the wild for fifty-four days, Brian learned to focus on and be more appreciative of the *present* (and, to a lesser degree, the future). This made him more observant and overall happier with his life. Next, Brian expectedly goes through significant changes in his *physique*, though these are never mentioned in the book. You know what they say: humans have incredible biological adaptability.

Related to how Brian's attitude toward life changes, the book also highlights the power of *positive thinking* (and encourages it). Once Brian started thinking positively, he achieved wonders in the wild. He was also able to recover from heartbreaking incidents—like his shelter getting blown away—surprisingly fast. Because Brian *believed* in success, he could *achieve* success. Along with learning from mistakes, *Hatchet* really drives home *how we should think about life*. No matter what, your plans can never be perfect. Sometimes, the only way to learn is to try and fail. And positive thinking will give us the strength to carry on.

The book also touches on the effect of *isolation* and *loneliness*. Before Brian's thoughts grow so strong, he had difficulties getting over failure. While it's true that Brian develops a thick skin from being alone, it significantly disturbs his mind as well. There were several instances (following devastating events) in the book where Brian attempted to take his own life. If he had someone to talk to, perhaps his thoughts would not have reached such dark spaces. This tells us the power of human relationship and how it supports us in our darkest hours.

Finally, let me make a short statement on *nature*. As the book illustrates, nature is nothing to be messed with. It's cruel, unforgiving, and cold—but is it *evil*? No. Consider carefully: nature never *actively* tries to harm or kill Brian. Whenever Brian experiences something unfortunate, it's more on him "being in the wrong place at the wrong time." At the same time, nature is neither *supportive*. Nature provides tools and resources for Brian to use for his survival—such as the animals he catches for food and the wood he uses to build his shelter. However, nature doesn't *actively* aid Brian by dispensing cooked fish or a fully-built shed directly in front of him. Accordingly, we may describe nature as cruel, unforgiving, coldhearted, or ruthless, but we can never assess it as *good* or *evil*.

1 Summary and First Impressions

A. Can you describe your favorite part of the story? Why do you like the part the most?

B. What do you think about the story? Do you like it?

2 Discussion Questions

A. In which moments during the story does Brian display an impressive understanding of nature?

> **Hint**
>
> Think of how and where he found shelter, how he found food, improved his armory, and interacted with hostile animals in the wild. To give you some examples, one of the first things he did was to harvest and consume berries from the forest. Berries are commonly known as the most available food to find in the wild. Next, Brian acts calm when he encounters a mature bear. He knows that as long as he stays out of its way and does not aggravate it, it won't turn hostile on him. Now, try to think of other instances throughout the story where Brian showed his wisdom and understanding of nature.

B. How does Brian's survival skills improve as the story continues? Why do they change?

> **Hint**
>
> Think of how Brian's hunting strategies changed. Also, think of how Brian's attitude toward resources (that he finds in the wild) changed. The more he survives, the more he adapts.

    i. Do you think anyone can survive like Brian if they were suddenly dropped in the wild?

C. How is nature drawn in this book? Is nature a good entity, an evil entity, or neither (i.e., indifferent) with respect to Brian? What do you think the author is trying to say about nature?

D. How does Brian's mind(set) change as he survives longer in the wild?

i. How is Brian affected by missing the airplane? How is Brian affected by the tornado blowing away his house? Are there any differences in how he reacts to the two events?

ii. Consider other critical events that Brian goes through as well (e.g., getting stung by a porcupine, getting sprayed by a skunk, getting rammed by a moose, dropping his hatchet in the river). Does his attitude (and his reaction) change toward these setbacks?

iii. How does Brian's change in attitude influence his life after he returns to the city?

E. After Brian returns to the city, what does he realize as the biggest difference between the life in the wild and the life in the city? For what element of the city life does he grow a humble appreciation?

    i. What do you think are the biggest differences between the life in the wild and the life in the city? What would be the most painful complication of living in the wild?

F. Do you think Brian eventually got to enjoy being alone in the woods? Do you think he would want to return to the forest and do it again?

G. How important was Brian's hatchet in his survival? What would have happened if he didn't have his hatchet?

    i. Do you suppose there's a better tool than a hatchet when surviving in the wild? What would it be?

H. At the end of the book, Brian decides against telling his father the "Secret." Why do you think he does so? Would he have been able to tell his father if he hadn't gone through his survival adventure?

I.   Do you think the story would have drastically changed if there was another survivor alongside Brian? How would have Brian turned out (differently) if he had a companion?

Vocabulary Exercise

Instructions

These are some words and phrases used in *Hatchet*. Write each of their definition in English. Then, write a paragraph with the topic of your liking using <u>at least seven</u> of these words/phrases. Be mindful that one word/phrase can have multiple meanings or be used in more than one way. Carefully consider how the words and phrases were used in the original book, and try to use each word/phrase the same way as how the book used it.

Words & Phrases

staggering (*adj.*)	gingerly	interior	diminish	ruefully
be in discomfort	audible	tender	initial	indicate

Sentences from the book

Here are the sentences from the original book that contains the given words. Only use these as reference and do not write the same sentences for your exercise.

staggering: … and after spending one night with the fire for a friend he knew what a **staggering** amount of wood it would take.

gingerly: His fingers **gingerly** touched a group of needles that had been driven through his pants and into the fleshy part of his calf.

interior: … the yellow and red flames brightening the dark **interior** of the shelter, …

diminish: … and he didn't want to **diminish** any chance he might have of being found.

ruefully: If only I had matches, he thought, looking **ruefully** at the beach and lakeside.

be in discomfort: Brian turned back to avoid embarrassing the pilot, who **was** obviously **in** some **discomfort**.

audible: "Don't know, kid …" The pilot's words were a hiss, barely **audible**.

tender: She nodded. "Just like a scout. My little scout." And there was the **tenderness** in her voice that she had when she was small …

initial: There had been the **initial** excitement, of course.

indicate: Down beneath that were dials with lines that seemed to **indicate** what the winds were doing, …

Paragraph Write-up Exercise

Instructions

Write a short paragraph expressing your thoughts about the following questions. There are multiple questions to guide you arrange your thoughts and form your answer. Be sure to answer all the questions within a single paragraph—do not answer the questions individually.

A "paragraph" is a collection of sentences (which are not divided into separate lines) that convey a single idea throughout. The sentences in a paragraph must be logically arranged to coherently deliver your thoughts to the reader. A single paragraph must contain at least three sentences.

Question

If you were to be stranded in an unmanned island, what would be the <u>three</u> things you would bring with you? Explain why for each. You may bring a living being (be it human or animal); one life counts as one choice.

Bibliography

About the Author

Gary James Paulsen (born Mar 17, 1939; died Oct 13, 2021, aged 82) was an American author born in Minnesota, U.S. His specialty was coming-of-age novels for children and young adults based on nature and the wild. His most well-known works include *Hatchet*, *Dogsong*, and *The Winter Room*.

https://www.penguinrandomhouse.com/authors/23384/gary-paulsen/

Other Books by the Author

Columns of each table: (from left) Title of Book; Year Published; ATOS Book Level; Lexile Measure; Interest Level.

Guide to Interest Level:

LG (Lower Grades; suitable for grades K-3)

MG (Middle Grades; suitable for grades 4-8)

MG+ (Middle Grades Plus; suitable for grades 6+)

UG (Upper Grades; suitable for grades 9-12)

Brian's Saga Series				
Hatchet *1988 Newbery Honor	1987	5.7	1020L	MG
The River (Hatchet: The Return)	1991	5.5	960L	MG
Brian's Winter (Hatchet: Winter)	1996	5.9	1140L	MG
Brian's Return (Hatchet: The Call)	1999	5.5	1030L	MG
Brian's Hunt	2003	5.9	1120L	MG+

Lawn Boy Series				
Lawn Boy	2007	4.3	710L	MG
Lawn Boy Returns	2010	5.6	920L	MG

Liar, Liar Series				
Liar, Liar: The Theory, Practice and Destructive Properties of Deception	2011	5.8	940L	MG
Flat Broke: The Theory, Practice and Destructive Properties of Greed	2011	5.1	810L	MG
Crush: The Theory, Practice and Destructive Properties of Love	2012	5.1	780L	MG
Vote: The Theory, Practice, and Destructive Properties of Politics	2013	5.5	820L	MG
Family Ties: The Theory, Practice, and Destructive Properties of Relatives	2014	5.5	840L	MG

Novels				
Tracker	1984	5.3	930L	MG
Dogsong *1986 Newbery Honor	1986	5.2	930L	MG
The Winter Room *1990 Newbery Honor	1989	5.0	1110L	MG
Woodsong	1990	5.6	1030L	MG
Harris and Me: A Summer Remembered	1993	5.7	980L	MG+
How Angel Peterson Got His Name	2003	6.0	1180L	MG
Notes from the Dog	2009	4.7	760L	MG
Mudshark	2009	6.3	1080L	MG
Masters of Disaster	2010	6.5	NC1100L	MG
Woods Runner	2010	5.5	870L	MG+

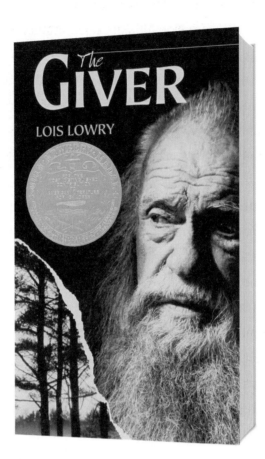

The Giver

---

by Lois Lowry

Published	1993 (1994 Newbery Medal)
ATOS Book Level	5.7
Lexile	760L
Word Count	43617

Imagine a world without war, hatred, pain, and poverty—tempting, isn't it? Now imagine the world is also deprived of color, emotion, choice, and memory. Is this a world in which you'd like to live? Are the sacrifices worth it? *The Giver* presents a future society with precisely these features. In this community, everyone looks and acts virtually the same; there is no competition, and everyone is polite. Any semblance of suffering has been eradicated, and a tranquil state called "Sameness" has been achieved. Unable to make choices, the community members have everything—their names, parents, siblings, spouses, and lifelong vocations—decided *for* them by their governors (the "Elders"). Like everyone else, Jonas, our hero, is designated his lifetime profession as he turns twelve—he becomes appointed as the next "Receiver of Memory." The Receiver tends to all the memories surrendered by the community members. Their main task is to advise the Elders in case of a problem by consulting similar events of the past. The Elders recognized this problem-solving power of memories and assigned exactly one community member as the caretaker. The current Receiver (a.k.a. "The Giver") is old, and a successor must be trained. Through the touch of The Giver, Jonas receives various memories—some delightful, but mostly painful—over repeated sessions. Astonishingly, receiving memories restores Jonas's abilities to see colors and feel emotions. With that, he starts to notice the community's flaws—he realizes that confiscating choice and memory was a mistake. To correct this mistake, Jonas plans to exit the community, which will release all his memories to its members. While he knows this will cause them agony, he believes this will be necessary to free the community from its chains. Will Jonas succeed in his plans?

Themes

The Giver is what I refer to as: "the perfect link between children's novels and classic novels." The scenario presented in this book resembles those you frequently encounter in the more advanced "classic novels." Many of these books—like *Brave New World* (Aldous Huxley), *1984* (George Orwell), *Fahrenheit 451* (Ray Bradbury), and *The Time Machine* (H. G. Wells)—love presenting an imaginary world with its own laws and features. As the reader, you are tasked to interpret and analyze the world and seek what benefits and problems it would contain. These books often offer a seemingly charming community with peace and order.

Yet, as you follow the story, you gradually realize that the world may not seem as perfect as it promotes itself. The deeper you delve into the plot, the more you fathom the faults and loopholes of the world. These cause problems, light conflicts, or even drive the world to a catastrophe at the climax—that's why these books are often referred to as "*dystopian* novels." In addition, just like *The Giver*, these books usually feature a protagonist who follows a similar process to you (the reader)—as the main character's understanding of the fictional world ripens, they begin to understand that the world is not as perfect as the other characters perceive. The main character struggles to persuade the others of their perspective until they eventually decide to devise a plan to overthrow the order. Jonas also has his own plan to disrupt the community and thereby educate its members, but we never get to see if it works out at the end of the book. That's because *The Giver* is part of a tetralogy—unfortunately, they all have mediocre reviews. You are welcome to try them out yourself, though.

Although breaking down such dystopian novels is complex, there are several reasons why *The Giver* is classified as a children's novel. The first is its language: compared to most of the classic novels mentioned above, *The Giver* uses easy wording suitable for children. The second—and the more important—is that the limitations and handicaps involved in *The Giver's* world are much more intuitable than those in some classic novels. Many classic novels present issues that are highly political, e.g., democracy vs. communism, the use of drugs to regulate people's behaviors, and the segregation of classes among people. Compared to these ideas, the issues handled in *The Giver* are more accessible to children—the absence of color, emotion, choice, and memory (and their consequences) are appropriate for children to assess. In conclusion, *The Giver* is an excellent link between children's novels and classic novels (which you *should* ultimately advance toward).

As noted, whenever you encounter a dystopian novel like *The Giver*, your job—as the reader—is to dissect the society within and compare its characteristics to the one we live in now. Let's perform this evaluation on *The Giver*. We will begin by examining the positive aspects. Most of them—such as the absence of war, hatred, pain, and poverty—goes without saying; we can intuit that all these are preferable without having to analyze them extensively. However, one element requires closer consideration: the automatic selection of your job. While I think everybody would appreciate the availability to choose their own profession, if the government laboriously examines your capabilities and provides the perfect role for you in society, it would undeniably be convenient. Not only will you enjoy your job (as it is theoretically perfect for you), but you will also not have to worry about getting fired, as it will be your lifelong profession.

Being a dystopian novel, however, *The Giver's* community holds a fair share of shortcomings. The first noteworthy missing feature is *color*. What would the world be like if all colors were to disappear? What would it be like to live in a grayscale world? First of all, it would be absolutely lifeless. Color breathes *life* into things. Each color makes us experience a unique set of emotions; two objects of the same shape but different colors can feel like two completely separate objects. Take *clothes* as an example. Two clothes of the same design but different colors sell variedly because of customer preferences and the color's harmony with the design. People favor different colors due to having distinct personalities. Even a single person's color preference may change depending on their mood. Here, we identify the relationship between *color* and *choice*—we make many choices *based on color* (e.g., what color clothes to wear, shoes to put on, and car to buy). Hence is why the elimination of color triggers the loss of choice. Above all, the lack of color perhaps most critically impacts *traffic lights*. The only factor that separates the different signals of a traffic light is color—that's why colorblind people are prohibited from driving. Without color, traffic lights would be pointless. And this is why *The Giver's* community doesn't have any traffic—there are no automated vehicles; everyone travels by bicycle.

What else do we not have? *Emotion.* Getting rid of emotion would have been pivotal in eradicating complex interpersonal problems—such as hatred, prejudice, discrimination, and violence. Negative emotion generated by the clash of diverged opinions is the prime cause of brawls (either verbal or physical) between people. But was it necessary to annihilate all human emotions? Was that the only way to keep the people in line? Imagine a world without emotions—everyone would act like robots. People will neither feel the need to compete nor improve. Society will arrive at an absolute halt—there will be no change, for either good or bad. Yet *change* is what keeps us going—the strive for improvement grants advanced technology and convenience. Without emotion, no one will be motivated to change; society could remain the same for hundreds of years. Isn't that a sad sight?

Next, we do not have *choice* in this community. Everything—down to your name—is decided by the Elders. A life without choice would be not only mundane but also never-improving. We're not always going to make the "right choice" in every instance of our lives. And even if you *thought* the "right choice" at the time, you might be dissatisfied with the outcome—you might regret making that choice. We learn from our mistakes—especially not to make the same disappointing choice again. If we cannot make choices for ourselves, we will never learn anything from life; we might make the same mistakes over and over again. We gain valuable lessons whenever we make a decision in our lives—whether we are satisfied with the result or not. The lack of *choice* is also related to the absence of *memory*. Our memory guides us in the right direction by compiling all our trials and errors. But if there are no "trials (making choices)," then there are also no "errors (mistakes)," and our memory will lose its critical function.

Lastly, the people of *The Giver* are short of *memory*. It isn't clear *how far back* one's memory reaches in the book. It says that people can remember what they did yesterday, but the elderly do not preserve the wisdom they gained throughout their working years. Still, we can be sure that no one in the community gets educated on *history*. Only The Giver and Jonas carry the memories of what the world was like *before Sameness*. We can find the significance of memory in why "The Receiver of Memory" position was instituted. While the Elders did not grant memory to the community members, they decided against completely erasing all memories—instead, they inaugurated a caretaker to tend to them. This was because the Elders realized the almighty problem-solving power of memories. Our memories precisely shine in this area: *solving problems*. Whenever you go through an event, it is converted to and saved as a memory in your mind. Memory becomes an experience from which we can extract knowledge and wisdom. We can use that wisdom to tackle future problems. At the same time, wisdom prevents us from making the same mistake again. As explained, remembering a regrettable choice from the past saves you from the same undesirable result. Wisdom also serves as a connection between the older generation and the younger generation. The most valuable aid the younger generation can gain from the older generation is their wisdom built up by their years of experience. However, the elderly in *The Giver* lack wisdom—that's why they're treated with no respect—just like little kids—until they are "released" (or *killed off*).

So now, after evaluating this community in depth, do you think it is worth it? Is this society what humanity should strive to achieve? Is this where we should be head to in the future?

Questions

① Summary and First Impressions

A. Can you describe your favorite part of the story? Why do you like the part the most?

B. What do you think about the story? Do you like it?

② Discussion Questions

A. Let's consider each of the virtues *missing* from *The Giver's* community, starting from *color*. What would it be like to live in a grayscale world, devoid of any color?

   i. What would be the most striking change that would take place in our lives if all colors disappeared? What would arise as the most critical issue if all colors disappeared?

> **Hint**
>
> Think of all the places where color is involved and plays an important role in our lives. When do you contemplate deeply over colors? Think of two (or more) things that would become indistinguishable (or meaningless to distinguish) if colors were to disappear. In which part of our lives is color the only definitive separator between mixed signals? Do some colors hold individual significance? Do some colors transmit particular messages or signals?

   ii. How is the lack of color related to the other absences (of emotion, entertainment, choice, and memory)?

   iii. Why do you think it was necessary to get rid of color to achieve Sameness and absolute peace?

B. Now, let's consider *emotions*. What would it be like to live in a world where no one feels any emotions?

  i. How would social interactions change? Would any human relationship (e.g., friendship, romantic relationship, family relationship) be meaningful anymore? What would arise as the most critical issue if all emotions disappeared?

  ii. How is the lack of emotions related to the other absences (color, entertainment, choice, and memory)?

  iii. Why do you think it was necessary to get rid of emotions to achieve Sameness and absolute peace?

C. Now let's think about *choices*. What would it be like to live in a world where you have no freedom to make your own choices?

i. A particular branch of "no choice" (in *The Giver*) we should investigate is that related to one's job. What do you think about having no choice in picking your job? If your personal skills and talents are carefully considered for the designation of your position, would you rather have your job chosen for you? Or would you still want to make the decision yourself?

ii. How is the lack of (the availability of) choice related to the other absences (of color, emotions, entertainment, and memory)?

iii. Why do you think it was necessary to get rid of choice to achieve Sameness and absolute peace?

D. Finally, *memory*. Note that, within the context of our discussion here, memory = history. Why do we learn history at school? Why is it important to know your country's history?

Chew on this

The citizen of any country must know the basics of their history. Proud moments infuse pride in their culture and awe in their ancestors' wisdom, while embarrassing moments ensure a similar event never occurs again. In particular, both schools and students must not shy away from investigating their country's *shameful* history. Learning it may be painful, but it's only temporary. In the long run, this will assure the upsetting history shall never be relived in the succeeding generations. An excellent example of this is how Germany educates its students on the Holocaust. I'll leave it to you to find out more about this.

---

i. How do you use your personal memories? Where do your memories come in handy?

Hint

Can your personal memories act in a similar way to a country's history? Is national history to a country as is personal memories to an individual?

---

ii. How does your personal memories affect you when you make a choice? How are choice and memory related?

iii. How are the personal memories of the elderly (i.e., the retirees) in this book? Do they carry vivid memories of their younger years? Why are they treated with no respect, like little kids?

E. The book states: should The Receiver of Memory be killed or discharged from the community, the influx of bad memories will cause pain and suffering to all the members. Notwithstanding this risk, the Committee of Elders has left one person to tend to all the memories. Why do you think the Elders decided to preserve all the memories instead of expunging them completely (especially if no one else than The Receiver of Memory will ever hold them)? Why does the community need at least one person alive with all the memories?

Hint

Consider what was discussed above regarding the function of history and the related role of personal memory. Why would the community need to keep hold of the memories? For which occasion would they use them?

F. Why does Jonas begin to get isolated from his friends (as well as the rest of the community) as the story proceeds? Is it related to his duties in any way?

G. In the strictly controlled community of *The Giver*, people's language is also regulated by a system called the "precision of language." Ironically, with this community missing so many elements, many words we frequently use in real life are rendered useless. What words and phrases would be meaningless in *The Giver's* world?

Hint

Think of all the things missing in *The Giver's* community—like color, emotions, pain, war, etc.

H. There are various traditions and customs in *The Giver's* community. For one, every community member's lifelong job gets chosen at the "Ceremony of Twelve." How do these customs affect the citizens? How do your culture's customs affect you? Are there any customs of other cultures that intrigue you?

Vocabulary Exercise

Instructions

These are some words and phrases used in *The Giver*. Write each of their definition in English. Then, write a paragraph with the topic of your liking using <u>at least seven</u> of these words/phrases. Be mindful that one word/phrase can have multiple meanings or be used in more than one way. Carefully consider how the words and phrases were used in the original book, and try to use each word/phrase the same way as how the book used it.

Words & Phrases

reassure	designate	unaccustomed	solemnly	reluctantly,
meticulously	amidst	self-conscious	discipline	utmost

Sentences from the book

Here are the sentences from the original book that contains the given words. Only use these as reference and do not write the same sentences for your exercise.

reassure: But his mother laughed again in a **reassuring**, affectionate way.

designate: The little girl nodded and looked down at herself, at the jacket with its row of large buttons that **designated** her as a Seven.

unaccustomed: He saw the Tens stroking their new shortened hair, the females shaking their heads to feel the **unaccustomed** lightness.

solemnly: She stood **solemnly** listening to the speech of firm instructions on the responsibilities of Eight and doing volunteer hours for the first time.

reluctantly: "... have you ever once known of anyone ... who joined another community?" / "No." Asher admitted **reluctantly**.

meticulously: The community was so **meticulously** ordered, the choices so carefully made.

amidst: Number one—her name was Madeline—returned, finally, **amidst** applause, to her seat ...

self-conscious: He paid strict attention as his friend went to the stage and stood **self-consciously** beside the Chief Elder.

discipline: The punishment used for small children was a regulated system of smacks with the **discipline** wand.

utmost: His mind reeled. Now, empowered to ask questions of utmost **rudeness** …

Paragraph Write-up Exercise

Instructions

Write a short paragraph expressing your thoughts about the following questions. There are multiple questions to guide you arrange your thoughts and form your answer. Be sure to answer all the questions within a single paragraph—do not answer the questions individually.

A "paragraph" is a collection of sentences (which are not divided into separate lines) that convey a single idea throughout. The sentences in a paragraph must be logically arranged to coherently deliver your thoughts to the reader. A single paragraph must contain at least three sentences.

Question

What is your version of the utopia (i.e., the perfect world)? What would be some things the people would have to surrender to achieve your utopia? What problems do you foresee in your utopia?

Bibliography

Lois Lowry (85; born Mar 20, 1937) is an American children and young-adults' author born in Hawaii, U.S. She specializes in weaving complex subject matters into her stories. She is also known for her writings about dystopias. Her most well-known works include *The Giver* series, *Number the Stars*, and *Rabble Starkey*.

https://loislowry.com/

Other Books by the Author

Columns of each table: (from left) Title of Book; Year Published; ATOS Book Level; Lexile Measure; Interest Level.

Guide to Interest Level:
LG (Lower Grades; suitable for grades K-3)
MG (Middle Grades; suitable for grades 4-8)
MG+ (Middle Grades Plus; suitable for grades 6+)
UG (Upper Grades; suitable for grades 9-12)

Giver Series				
The Giver *1994 Newbery Medal	1993	5.7	760L	MG
Gathering Blue	2000	5.0	680L	MG+
Messenger	2004	4.9	720L	MG+
Son	2012	5.0	720L	MG+

Sam Krupnik Series				
All About Sam	1988	4.0	670L	MG
Attaboy, Sam	1992	4.6	740L	MG
See You Around, Sam!	1996	4.4	740L	MG
Zooman Sam	1999	4.1	680L	MG

Just the Tates! Series

The One Hundredth Thing About Caroline	1983	4.6	690L	MG
Switcharound	1985	4.6	680L	MG
Your Move, J.P.!	1990	4.9	750L	MG

Willoughbys Series

The Willoughbys	2008	5.2	790L	MG
The Willoughbys Return	2020	4.8		MG

Anastasia Krupnik Series

Anastasia Krupnik	1979	4.5	700L	MG
Anastasia Again!	1981	4.5	700L	MG
Anastasia at Your Service	1982	4.3	670L	MG
Anastasia, Ask Your Analyst	1984	4.2	630L	MG
Anastasia on Her Own	1985	4.4	640L	MG
Anastasia Has the Answers	1986	4.9	760L	MG
Anastasia's Chosen Career	1987	4.5	730L	MG
Anastasia at This Address	1991	4.6	730L	MG
Anastasia, Absolutely	1995	4.7	780L	MG

Novels

A Summer to Die	1977	5.3	800L	UG
Find A Stranger, Say Goodbye	1978	4.8	780L	UG
Autumn Street	1980	5.1	810L	MG
Taking Care of Terrific	1983	5.3	840L	MG
Rabble Starkey	1987	5.3	940L	MG
Number the Stars *1990 Newbery Medal	1989	4.5	670L	MG
Stay! Keeper's Story	1997	6.4	880L	MG
The Silent Boy	2003	5.1	870L	MG
Gossamer	2006	4.4	660L	MG
Crow Call (picture books)	2009	3.8	AD750L	LG
The Birthday Ball	2010	5.2	810L	MG
Bless this Mouse	2011	4.5	690L	LG

Nonfiction				
Looking Back: A Book of Memories	1998	5.5	900L	MG
On the Horizon: World War II Reflections	2020	4.2	HL580L	MG

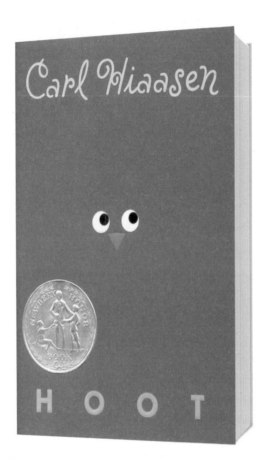

Hoot

by Carl Hiaasen

Published	2002 (2003 Newbery Honor)
ATOS Book Level	5.2
Lexile	760L
Word Count	61113

W ildlife is a blessing—it is fascinating to observe and interact with. Unfortunately, it is rapidly slipping through our fingers as civilization evolves. Any remaining wildlife must, therefore, be protected at all costs. Our hero today perfectly understands this predicament. Meet Roy Eberhardt, a new kid in Coconut Cove, Florida. Although he has just moved in, he is well aware of the famous TV star's upcoming restaurant, Mother Paula's Pancake House— which is under construction in town right now. However, Roy has no time to pay attention to that. All his interests are set on the mysterious running boy he first witnessed on his way to school. Through an overwhelming number of adversities, Roy finally confronts the running boy. The boy goes by his nickname, "Mullet Fingers," and is the stepbrother of Beatrice Leep, Roy's schoolmate. Apparently, Mullet Fingers—who is the same age as Roy—has dropped out of school due to a conflict with his mother. While wandering around the wild, he got engrossed in Mother Paula's construction site, which happens to contain a burrowing owl nest. Mullet Fingers has tried everything he can to protect the owls—from pulling out the survey stakes to putting alligators into the porta potties. Despite all his efforts, the construction persists, and it seems like Mother Paula's is set to open anytime soon. Roy learns about the owls when he finds Mullet Fingers injured at the construction site after another failed vandalism attempt. Now, Roy decides to help Mullet Fingers to stop the construction. However, unlike Mullet Fingers, Roy plans a protest at the opening ceremony. He asks for his classmates' help and gathers proof of the owls' presence. Will Roy and Mullet Fingers successfully stop the construction and save the owls?

Themes

T aking the story as a whole, an apparent theme is *protecting wildlife*. Ever since the surfacing of human civilization, wildlife has been suffering from pollution and losing its precious habitats. The International Union for Conservation of Nature (IUCN) Red List estimates that approximately 900 species have gone extinct since 1500 due to human interference. To make matters worse, countless species on earth are presumed to be still awaiting discovery—this means that there are likely many species that have gone extinct *under our radar*. *Numerous* topics are related to wildlife protection—including industrialization, global warming, and deforestation. However, most of these are beyond the scope of this book.

Hoot puts forward the idea of how big-name companies customarily *overlook* wildlife protection. Admittedly, a company, by definition, denotes a group of people working toward communal profit. Nevertheless, the pursuit of profit must always be within the boundaries of legitimacy. Never should a company neglect the law for its benefit. Unfortunately, it is challenging for an individual to directly tackle a company. However, there are ways to prevent malicious companies from ruining wildlife—we could hold protests against them (like Roy did in the story) or inform our local policymakers. Not only should we, as individuals, try our best to preserve nature, but we should also keep an eye out for others' sinister attempts to harm nature for their interests.

A relatively obscure theme of the book is *education*. In *Hoot*, we get two contradicting characters: Roy and Mullet Fingers are aged the same, but only Roy attends school. Correspondingly, we witness a decisive disparity between the boys' approaches toward resolving the burrowing owl issue. Mullet Fingers selected vandalism as his weapon—he disturbs the construction site in various ways to halt the operation. Some of his acts are purely annoying—like pulling out the survey stakes and making truck tires flat—but some are dangerous—like putting alligators in porta potties. In fact, Mullet Fingers eventually hurts himself while carrying out one of his stunts—he gets attacked by the construction site guard dogs. Let alone being dangerous, all of Mullet Fingers' actions were illegal. Inflicting damage upon someone else's property, causing injury to others, and interfering with a police investigation—are all blatant crimes. Had Roy not stepped in to help Mullet Fingers, he would have likely been apprehended by the police. On the other hand, Roy chose a peaceful protest as his weapon. His approach was to gather evidence to prove the presence of the burrowing owls on the construction site and showcase the ignorance and recklessness of the operation to the public. The "gathering evidence" part involved some complications, but in the end, Roy's plan succeeded in stopping the construction. The power of his classmates' conjoined voices managed to open the public's eye to the threatened wildlife, and they earned the public's approval to terminate the construction.

So, how does this difference between Mullet Fingers' and Roy's efforts to resolve the owl issue relate to their *education*? Since Mullet Fingers didn't attend school, he couldn't brainstorm a peaceful and efficient way of solving the problem—the concept of a demonstration was not present in his brain. Instead, the only thing he could conjure up was to disrupt the construction physically —which is a rather shortsighted strategy. (We can't blame him for this, though.) In contrast, Roy, who attends school, was able to propose the proper, gentle way of untangling the issue. It's unlikely that his school precisely instructs him to solve such problems with peaceful protests. But history, social studies, and other subjects will tell him that precarious social issues have often been settled through demonstrations in the past. Using this knowledge, Roy devised, organized, and carried out a peaceful protest—which hit the mark.

However, just because Roy is the only one who went to school, it doesn't mean Roy is conclusively more intelligent than Mullet Fingers. For one, Mullet Fingers has much richer knowledge about nature. (And he's also way better at catching mullets with bare hands.) School and general education provide the minimum knowledge and skills you need to pursue a stable life within society. Elaborate, specific knowledge must be obtained through personal endeavors. Mandatory education (up to either middle school or high school, depending on the country) would be undeniably beneficial to receive. But tertiary education could be optional. Learning expert knowledge from the professionals (the professors) in the area you're interested in would grant you a comfortable start to your career. However, sometimes, the hands-on experience could be more precious than learning from others; in some fields, people with long experience outperform those who've just come out of professional training. Think about why you go to school, what you expect to gain from school, and how it could be different from not going to school.

Now, time for some final minor topics. Roy displays powerful *friendship* and *loyalty* as he lends his name to Mullet Fingers when registering him at the hospital. He knows he will get into trouble for deception, but he cares more about his friend's well-being than his punishment. Here, we find another notable theme—*lying*. Roy lies for Mullet Fingers' safety—is this okay to do? Is lying okay if you have good intentions? In addition, aren't "good intentions" subjective? (Remember *Shiloh*?) Finally, *misbehaviors and morality*. Roy does not participate in Mullet Fingers' vandalism saga, but he doesn't stop him either. As long as he is not directly involved, Roy disregards Mullet Fingers doing his thing, although he knows well that everything he does is illegal. Does Roy have any responsibility for Mullet Fingers' actions? Should he have actively stopped Mullet Fingers?

Questions

① Summary and First Impressions

A. Can you describe your favorite part of the story? Why do you like the part the most?

B. What do you think about the story? Do you like it?

② Discussion Questions

A. Just like in the book, many real-life human activities often threaten wildlife (big or small, legal or illegal, and intentional or unintentional). What do you think we can do to protect wildlife?

   i. What can you do, as an individual, to help protect wildlife?

   ii. What should a government do to protect its country's wildlife?

   iii. Why is it important to protect wildlife?

B. Mullet Fingers, when he learned about the owls' presence, tried to stop the construction by vandalizing the site. He flattened the truck tires, pulled out survey stakes, stole the bulldozer seat, etc. What do you think about Mullet Fingers' approach to stopping the operation? Was it effective? Are his actions legal? Can his actions be justified in such a case?

> **Chew on this**
>
> Mullet Fingers' strategy to stop the construction was to vandalize (i.e., physically hurt) the site. To give him some credit, he did manage to slow down the operation. However, his approach ultimately failed—his acts of vandalism only delayed the construction but never terminated it. The construction got back on track when Mullet Fingers hurt himself during one of his stunts and could no longer continue his interruptions. Furthermore, vandalism is illegal—you cannot damage others' properties and assets. Mullet Fingers got lucky not getting caught by the police. Had he been caught, he would have been sent straight to jail. Criminal behavior cannot be justified under any circumstance. Even if your opponent breaks the law, you need to fight fair to give them the punishment they deserve. If you break the law to fight people who break the law, you just become one of them.

    i.   Do you think Mullet Fingers' strategy would be effective in real life in such a situation (i.e., to stop a corporate project)? Do you think his strategy is legitimate?

C. Roy—when he learned about the owls through Mullet Fingers—tried to stop the construction by holding a peaceful protest. He gathered his classmates, got some legal help from his dad, and held his campaign at the opening ceremony. What do you think about Roy's approach to stopping the operation? Was it effective? Are his actions legal?

Chew on this

Roy's strategy to stop the construction was to hold a peaceful protest. He persuaded his friends to participate and tried to gather evidence for the owls' presence on the construction site. Although he had trouble in the "gathering evidence" department, his plan still successfully stopped the operation and saved the owls. With enough voices conjoined, Roy's efforts saw the light of day and received support from the public. What's also important is that he kept it peaceful from the beginning to the end. Not only was his approach effective, but it was also absolutely legitimate.

---

    i.   Do you think Roy's strategy would be effective in real life in such a situation (i.e., to stop a corporate project)? Do you think his strategy is legitimate?

D. Other than Mullet Fingers' and Roy's approaches, do you think there is another (perhaps an even better) way to resolve the owl issue?

E. In the book, Mullet Fingers dropped out of school and pursued what caught his attention (i.e., the burrowing owl issue) instead. Do you think this is okay? If you found an activity you'd like to focus on, do you think it's okay to quit school during your teens?

    i.   Considering your current interests, which activity/topic would be the one to make you leave school? Which activity/topic would most likely prime you to quit school?

F. As Roy goes to school and Mullet Fingers doesn't, can we say that Roy is decisively more intelligent and skilled in every area of life compared to Mullet Fingers? Is Roy better than Mullet Fingers at everything?

G. Why was only Roy able to brainstorm the idea of holding a peaceful protest? Why could Mullet Fingers not think of such an idea? Is it related to him missing out on education?

i. What would have happened had Roy never joined Mullet Fingers? Had Mullet Fingers kept on trying to stop the construction all by himself, how would have the book ended?

H. Why do you think we need to go to school? Why do you think we need to receive general education? What would happen without school?

Instructions

These are some words and phrases used in *Hoot*. Write each of their definition in English. Then, write a paragraph with the topic of your liking using <u>at least seven</u> of these words/phrases. Be mindful that one word/phrase can have multiple meanings or be used in more than one way. Carefully consider how the words and phrases were used in the original book, and try to use each word/phrase the same way as how the book used it.

Words & Phrases

vandalize	surveillance	thoroughly	anticipation	unnoticed
exaggerate	interject	apprehend	triumphant	devotes

Sentences from the book

Here are the sentences from the original book that contains the given words. Only use these as reference and do not write the same sentences for your exercise.

vandalize: "A Coconut Cove police cruiser was **vandalized** early Monday morning …"

surveillance: "… he is part of a special **surveillance** team investigating property crimes …"

thoroughly: Officer Delinko was **thoroughly** confused.

anticipation: Once again he reached for his radio in **anticipation** of calling headquarters.

unnoticed: Beatrice Leep was gone and when Roy awoke. He had no idea how she had slipped out of the house **unnoticed**, but he was glad she'd made it.

exaggerate: "Whatever." Roy knew that Garrett was famous for **exaggerating**.

interject: Gruffly, the sergeant **interjected**: "Aw, the kid's jerking our chain, is all."

apprehend: "… I intend to tell Chief Deacon that the Mother Paula's vandal has been **apprehended**."

triumphant: "Owls!" Roy proclaimed **triumphantly**.

devote: Roy couldn't believe how much space the newspaper had **devoted** to the owl protest.

Paragraph Write-up Exercise

Instructions

Write a short paragraph expressing your thoughts about the following questions. There are multiple questions to guide you arrange your thoughts and form your answer. Be sure to answer all the questions within a single paragraph—do not answer the questions individually.

A "paragraph" is a collection of sentences (which are not divided into separate lines) that convey a single idea throughout. The sentences in a paragraph must be logically arranged to coherently deliver your thoughts to the reader. A single paragraph must contain at least three sentences.

Question

How do you think the book would have ended had Mullet Fingers never met Roy and had Roy never known about the owls? How important is it that Roy received general education (i.e., went to school)?

Bibliography

1 – "Biodiversity" from *Our World in Data* (https://ourworldindata.org/extinctions)

About the Author

Carl Hiaasen (69; born Mar 12, 1953) is an American author and journalist born in Florida, U.S. He started his career as a newspaper reporter, and he started writing children's and adults' novels in the 1970s. He specializes in the (often satirical) crime thriller genre. His most well-known works include *Hoot*, *Flush*, and *Chomp*.

http://www.carlhiaasen.com/

Other Books by the Author

Columns of each table: (from left) Title of Book; Year Published; ATOS Book Level; Lexile Measure; Interest Level.

Guide to Interest Level:

LG (Lower Grades; suitable for grades K-3)

MG (Middle Grades; suitable for grades 4-8)

MG+ (Middle Grades Plus; suitable for grades 6+)

UG (Upper Grades; suitable for grades 9-12)

Novels				
Hoot *2003 Newbery Honor	2002	5.2	760L	MG
Flush	2005	5.0	770L	MG
Scat	2009	5.5	810L	MG
Chomp	2012	5.2	800L	MG
Skink: No Surrender	2014	5.2	770L	MG+
Squirm	2018	4.9	740L	MG

Newbery Book Club

24 Award-Winning Novels with Matriductive Learners

엄마표 영어로 인풋이 안정된 친구들을 위한 뉴베리 북클럽

초판 1쇄 인쇄 2023년 4월 15일
초판 1쇄 발행 2023년 4월 25일

지은이 AJ(안재환)

대표 장선희 **총괄** 이영철
기획편집 현미나, 한이슬, 정시아
디자인 김효숙, 최아영 **외주디자인** 이창욱
마케팅 최의범, 임지윤, 김현진, 이동희
경영관리 김유미

펴낸곳 서사원 **출판등록** 제2021-000194호
주소 서울시 영등포구 당산로 54길 11 상가 301호
전화 02-898-8778 **팩스** 02-6008-1673
이메일 cr@seosawon.com
네이버 포스트 post.naver.com/seosawon
페이스북 www.facebook.com/seosawon
인스타그램 www.instagram.com/seosawon

ⓒAJ(안재환), 2023

ISBN 979-11-6822-171-0 13740

서사원은 독자 여러분의 책에 관한 아이디어와 원고 투고를 설레는 마음으로 기다리고 있습니다. 책으로 엮기를 원하는 아이디어가 있는 분은 이메일 cr@seosawon.com으로 간단한 개요와 취지, 연락처 등을 보내주세요. 고민을 멈추고 실행해 보세요. 꿈이 이루어집니다.